ON STYLE

ON STYLE

Inspiration and Advice

from the

New Generation of

Interior Design

CARL DELLATORE

RIZZOLI
NEW YORK

New York Paris London Milan

CONTENTS

INTRODUCTION

When talking about design, some critics say, "We have seen everything before. There's really nothing new being created." On a granular level, I'm inclined to agree.

But interior design has always been defined by its moment in time, generational movements that are, in turn, shaped by culture, economics, and fashion. For example, in the 1970s industrial minimalism was au courant. In the early 1980s, many decorators were putting their own spin on British or French design. Concurrently, other designers created rooms that celebrated juxtaposition: Lucite with floral chintz; streamlined Parsons tables with eighteenth-century Irish chairs. This set the stage for the eclecticism of the high-flying 1990s.

The rise of the Internet at the turn of the twenty-first century provided a proliferation of visual information to drive the eclectic movement still further. Glorious Moroccan color palettes, sleek midcentury Italian silhouettes, and the patina associated with Japanese *wabi-sabi* are just a few of the ideas designers freely incorporated into their work. With so many concepts in the mix, interior design increasingly became reflective of a global view.

That brings me to this book.

In choosing fifty designers who represent the next generation of interior design, I began by doing research. Who has great style? Who has something visually interesting to say? Who is moving the discipline forward?

As I sifted through the finalists, I found that there was no one style of design that captured today's moment. Instead, in what feels like a natural progression from eclecticism, there is a proliferation of aesthetic diversity. Words like *contemporary* or *classic* feel too limiting. We need a broader vocabulary to

In this stylish entry by Wesley Moon, a large, highly kinetic, and colorful painting by Ashley Chase Andrews lightens the more somber paneled walls. The bronze bench, by Timothy Schreiber from Wexler Gallery, gives the space a good shot of contemporary sculpture as furniture. The golden silk carpet is by Damien Langlois-Meurinne.

OVERLEAF: A collection of blue-and-white Delft porcelain plates is hung on the paneled and painted walls in this expansive dining room designed by Sarah Bartholomew. More blue touches appear on the chair upholstery and in delphiniums as centerpieces. The chunky textured rug is balanced by the more formal chandelier and sconces.

Moss greens, watery blues, sandstone, and black meld together to create a room, designed by Seattle-based Brian Paquette, that draws its color scheme from nature.

OVERLEAF: This loft by Kevin Dumais is organized around warm and cool neutral colors, with a layering of textures set against freshly painted white brick and pale gray oak floors. The finishes provide a calm backdrop for the remarkable exposed-timber ceiling. The linear pattern of the ceiling is mirrored in the large area rug from the Rug Company, which grounds the living room furniture and creates a fun dynamic between the two planes. The elm wood–and-acrylic coffee table emphasizes the play of materials used throughout the apartment and the balance of texture, weight, and lightness.

describe design today. Among the designers featured in this book, there are the New Traditionalists, who pay homage to classic design while responding to societal changes; the Modern Minimalists, who seek to create sanctuary to balance frenetic lives; the Saturated Colorists who conjure new palettes; the Casual Bohemians, who mix humble furnishings in exciting ways; and devotees of masculine restraint and urban chic.

Now, make no mistake: interior design's function will always be to provide a personal backdrop for the business of living, and Louis Sullivan's famous "form follows function" edict remains prescient. But there's a new freedom in interior design. We may have seen it all before, but the variety of aesthetic lenses through which designers see interiors is expanding exponentially and in tandem with the technological advances of the twenty-first century.

As you read the profiles of the fifty designers included in this book, with their thoughts on their influences and inspiration, color and key elements, it's my sincere hope that their answers, in concert with stylish images of their work, will inspire and delight you. Because in the end, isn't that what great design is all about?

THE PRINCIPALS

"A home's furnishings and objects should give the impression of being collected over time."

MICHAEL ADAMS

For Massachusetts native Michael Adams, a well-designed home is the backdrop, repository, and inspiration for family memories. This strong connection to family can be traced to his own, both sides of which arrived in the American colonies around 1620. Adams has a wealth of family stories: when he was eleven, he asked his mother about two early American Windsor chairs that resided in their kitchen. In December 1917, New England was hit with a record deep freeze. Temperatures held steady from minus 45 degrees in Maine to minus 16 in Rhode Island. Adams's great-great grandmother ran out of wood and was forced to use four of the chairs to fuel the fireplace. Two chairs survived to tell the story.

Yet don't expect to see an early American aesthetic in Adams's rooms. His vision for a successful space is rooted in eclecticism, a strong color sensibility, and thoughtfully considered furnishings. "Perfecting the right harmonious mixture of elements that, at the risk of sounding clichéd, make a house into a home is incredibly fulfilling," he says. "That my work will be the backdrop for memories is why I love my job."

Broad brushstrokes of color make this loft living room warm and inviting, while the streamlined shapes of the furnishings provide ample space for family and friends to gather. The books on the coffee table create a connection to the library in the back of the space.

FROM: Athol, Massachusetts

LOCATED IN: New York, New York

INFLUENCES: My inspiration is as varied and eclectic as the elements that I use. A single room can find inspiration from both Albert Hadley and Tim Burton or Eero Saarinen and Tony Duquette. While growing up in Massachusetts around early American antiques, I was able to live among furniture that was simple in its construction and materials but elegant and crude at the same time. I appreciate and anticipate how things will age.

ABOVE: A cool, monochromatic palette of grays sets a calming tone for this bedroom. The effect is amplified by floor-to-ceiling sheer curtains that create a cocoon-like bed. Antique Venetian mirrors add a touch of glamour. (left) The orderly color-coded bookshelves stand in juxtaposition to the Saarinen chairs and ottomans in this home library, while the Biedermeier cabinet provides another counterpoint. (right)

OPPOSITE: A Miles Aldridge photograph informs the color palette in this invigorating breakfast room. A brilliant yellow banquette contrasts with fluid chairs to complete the tableau.

THE LOOK: Thoughtful, fun, bold, whimsical.

COLOR: I use bold gestures of color with an interior shell of contrasting black and white tones that anchor the architecture. At the end, adding an object that is a wee bit acidic or sweet to each room activates the original color. An ocher Murano vase in a room with accents of pale flesh or robin's-egg blue serves as an accelerant for the color palette.

KEY ELEMENT: Scale. Before I talk about specific design details, I first figure out the need and function for each space and draft it, much like a coloring book. I can always add color and even pattern inside and outside the lines, but I always know where those lines are.

ALWAYS HAVE: After a space is complete and filled with its hard and soft finishes, I think adding a moment of abstraction, which could be a sculpture or a large plant, is important.

INSPIRATION: Visiting Doris Duke's Shangri La in Hawaii was as affecting as seeing Henry David Thoreau's one-room cabin on Walden Pond.

NEVER FORGET: The contrast and interplay created by the different elements of a room's design are as important as the elements themselves. A perfect minimal kitchen is more easily recognized as such with an imperfect antique in it. A soft-hued pink room can easily look like a giant lifeless Necco Wafer, so add a small shot of acid green and the pink vibrates with energy but without sacrificing the softness of cotton candy.

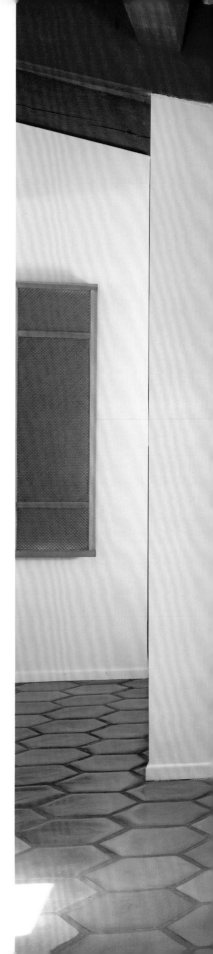

"Rooms should support an ease in living."

NATASHA BARADARAN

Natasha Baradaran spent childhood summers visiting her grandfather in Italy. A Persian antique-rug dealer, he moved to Milan with his family in the 1950s. Baradaran's multicultural background inspires her work, which mixes European design traditions, Middle Eastern exoticism, and the laid-back luxury of Los Angeles. In both her interiors and her furniture designs, she makes bold visual statements by thoughtfully juxtaposing materials and finishes.

Having started her career in design with an internationally renowned hospitality-design firm, Baradaran has worked on a range of commercial projects from casinos in Las Vegas to spas in South Korea. It was an experience that allowed her to apprentice with a group of very talented and tenured interior designers, including Joan Behnke. It was there that Baradaran learned how to structure projects, and how to stay on budget—skills she employed when establishing her eponymous firm in 2000.

FROM: Los Angeles, California

LOCATED IN: Los Angeles, California

INFLUENCES: Italian architecture and design as a whole serves as a major influence in my interiors and furniture designs. My favorite designers are Gio Ponti and Piero Portaluppi, who both happen to be Milanese. I love Ponti for the timelessness of his designs; his pieces and interiors are as relevant today as they were when he first created them. Also, I connect with him since he created not only spaces, but also original pieces to fit into his interiors. Portaluppi's sense of color, scale, and detail is a constant source of inspiration.

THE LOOK: Cool and internationally inflected.

A 1960s Venetian snowflake pendant hangs above a Saarinen table and director's chairs with Lucite backs in this breakfast room. Mismatched framed works are hung salon-style on the brick wall.

COLOR: I love color, and I would say that my color sensibilities come from my childhood in Milan. I love colors that are typically Milanese: terra-cotta, deep blue, and olive green. They are timeless, yet fresh at the same time. They inspire my interiors.

KEY ELEMENT: Sculptural lighting. It anchors a space for me, and then I work around that. It's art with function.

ALWAYS HAVE: A conversation starter piece to anchor a room. I love Hervé Van der Straeten's works in particular.

INSPIRATION: Even though Italy is most evident in my work, I am inspired by all the places I visit. An exposed tree trunk in Bora Bora gave me an idea for a table base. My time in Japan pushed me toward a less cluttered aesthetic. Family is a constant source, too. I have two daughters, and I have experimented with my own home and how I can live in a comfortable and relaxed environment while not sacrificing a refined and sophisticated feel. Fashion is another catalyst for inspiration: I love fashion, and I'm always interested in adapting its vocabulary to interiors.

NEVER FORGET: *Dolce far niente* is an Italian phrase that I come back to time and time again. It means the sweetness of doing nothing and the sheer indulgence of enjoying the moment. More than an expression, it's a way of life in Italy and a feeling that I have admired through the works of Federico Fellini.

TOP: In the home's great room, sophisticated neutral textiles creates a breezy, casual vibe.

CENTER: In the master bedroom, Rebecca Atwood's Marbled Stripe wallpaper in lilac hangs behind a glamorous Lucite bed.

BOTTOM: Custom neon signs dress up the pool deck.

OPPOSITE: This stylish Los Angeles entryway features a raffia-wrapped console from the 1970s and smoke-colored Murano table lamps.

SARAH BARTHOLOMEW

Sarah Bartholomew remembers when her mother first allowed her to decorate her room as a child. She chose a white wicker headboard; a blue, white, and green Laura Ashley print for the bedding; and a pale blue paint color for the walls.

Bartholomew grew up in Virginia outside of Washington, D.C., and developed a deep love for classical architecture and design at a young age. One of her earliest memories is of visiting Monticello as a child and being completely enchanted with the beauty of the interiors.

Bartholomew's designs are soft and inviting, inflected with traditional details. There's something immediately accessible about her rooms—they are spaces that beckon visitors to come in, sit down, and relax. And her color palettes are as fresh as the cut flowers you'll find in her home in Nashville.

with almost any color as long as it is incorporated in a fresh, edited way.

KEY ELEMENT: Pattern. It's often the source of inspiration for a room. Whether it is the pattern of an antique Oushak, a favorite textile, a chinoiserie piece of furniture, or a special piece of porcelain, it often gets the design process going.

ALWAYS HAVE: Myrtle topiaries. Layers. A dose of natural texture. At least one piece of contemporary art that the client has collected. A touch of blue.

INSPIRATION: Jefferson's Monticello embodies classical architecture. I could visit again and again and still learn more each visit. The Met and the Frick museums in New York and the Musée d'Orsay in Paris. Twentieth-century abstract artists usually inspire me most: Ellsworth Kelly, Agnes Martin, Cy Twombly, and Mark Rothko.

NEVER FORGET: How people lived in the past. Look at antique textiles, books, and literature—they are all sources of inspiration.

FROM: Washington, D.C.

LOCATED IN: Nashville, Tennessee

INFLUENCES: Renzo Mongiardino, Hubert de Givenchy, Thomas Jefferson, Albert Hadley, Syrie Maugham, Elsie de Wolfe, and Bill Blass—each inimitable and a genius in his or her own right.

THE LOOK: Thoughtfully curated and rooted in tradition, yet approachable.

COLOR: I have always gravitated toward blues, greens, and light, fresh neutrals— the colors most frequently seen in nature. In my work, I select the palette based on colors a client is drawn to. I can work

The silhouette of this antique Anglo-Indian bench (found at the Brimfield Antique Show) creates a graphic moment, even though the elements of the vignette are all traditional. It's the epitome of refined classicism. A series of engravings framed in French mats coordinate with the walls and bench cushion to tie the scheme together.

OPPOSITE: A grand moment is found in the room connecting the formal living and dining rooms. It's composed of a bullion-fringed table skirt, a custom Pierre Frey banquette, a vignette of decorative wall brackets, and antique hand-colored botanical prints. The room is grounded by a custom Swedish rug with marigold, blue, and green.

TOP: A sophisticated man's retreat was the idea behind this wood-paneled study. Warm, handsome textures and patterns with sumptuous windowpane-checked curtains play off custom chairs covered in a stronger palette and a casual weave.

CENTER: The incredible custom Iksel wallcovering is the star of this dining room. To maximize the decorative nature of the space, an antique chinoiserie étagère with incredible inlay fit the bill, along with a hand-blocked print for the drapery and a small-scale woven fabric for the dining chairs. This is a room where more is more!

BOTTOM: Lining the walls of the living room in a subtle marigold ticking stripe gave a warm, inviting air to the great space. This color was the foundation of the room, and the fabrics, furnishings, and art fell into place after that.

"Furnishings that appeal to you individually will undoubtedly work well together."

NEAL BECKSTEDT

Neal Beckstedt's aesthetic was formed during his childhood in Ohio's farmland. When he was seven, his family renovated their home, igniting Beckstedt's interest in design and architecture. He mused over the floor plans and eventual furniture placement. Beckstedt's family recognized and supported his creativity, and a career in design was born.

Fast-forward to his time enrolled in the College of Architecture and Planning at Ball State University, in Indiana, when Beckstedt was exposed to a wide range of influences, especially while spending a year in Italy. After moving to New York in 2000, he worked for an established architect, completing several projects before opening his own studio in 2010. Clean-lined forms, grounded in function over decoration, are the hallmark of his work.

FROM: Celina, Ohio

LOCATED IN: Brooklyn, New York

INFLUENCES: I'm particularly influenced by farm-building vernacular after being raised on a farm, especially the ideas of purism espoused by the Amish. I also appreciate the casualness of Danish design. Two designers I admire most are Jean-Michel Frank, a master, and Mies van der Rohe, one of the giants of modernist architecture.

THE LOOK: Casual, edited, effortless.

COLOR: As an architect, I rarely think about color first. I'm more concerned with form and volume. So I take my clues from my clients, who almost always have some digital information—Pinterest or Instagram—as a reference. I've been

For a couple with individual design visions in this downtown New York City triplex, a bright teal tufted sofa was designed for the lady of the house, while the nubby linen sofa was for the gentleman. The curtains accentuate the room's height, and the canvas between the windows is by artist Christopher Wool.

experimenting with and pushing the boundaries of color recently, which is something clients are asking me to do.

KEY ELEMENT: In designing a room, I almost always begin with the rug, often an antique.

ALWAYS HAVE: Texture. A carefully considered mix of textures is of real importance to me. Nubby wools, mohairs, leathers, wood grain, hair-on hides: disparate elements mixed in an eclectic way can create an electric spark in a room.

INSPIRATION: Getting out of my own element. Recently, I traveled to Madrid and Seville in Spain—I was intrigued by the antiquity and the mash-up of Islam and Christianity.

NEVER FORGET: Take chances, and mix it up. Pay attention to your personal likes and dislikes. If you love a ceramic lamp, buy it. Don't worry about bringing together elements.

TOP: A set of Mies van der Rohe chairs from Knoll are arranged around a Jean-Michel Frank table in this combined kitchen and dining area. The playful chandelier was chosen as a counterpoint to the linear furnishings.

CENTER: Hans Wegner's Papa Bear chair sits on the corner of a vintage Moroccan rug. The view into the powder room offers a glimpse of its silver-tinted wallpaper. (left) The master bedroom's wooden headboard drew its inspiration from the textured kilim rug. The artwork is by British artist James Nares. (right)

BOTTOM: The fireplace in this family room is flanked by two chunky ocher club chairs that contrast perfectly with the olive-green flatweave rug. The coffee table is custom made with a matte silver-leaf finish.

OPPOSITE: At the base of the stairs sit a vintage Pierre Jeanneret chair and a potter's stand found in Paris and repurposed as a side table. An overscale green glass lamp completes the vignette.

DELIA KENZA BRENNEN

New York–based interior designer Delia Kenza Brennen has had an interest in design for as long as she can remember.

Named after her much-loved grandmother, Brennen remembers how elegant her namesake was, both in how she dressed and how she lived. Brennen says, "My grandmother was a seamstress by trade, and she surrounded herself with beauty. While she didn't have much money, she had exquisite taste." Looking at Brennen's interiors, one can see the influence.

When working with her clients, Brennen strives for an emotional connection to her interiors; in fact, when her clients get that "feel-good energy," she knows she did their space justice. "The best rooms feel effortless," Brennen says. "When a space feels right, that's the golden moment. There is an automatic effortless ease and a level of comfort and warmth that does not feel forced or contrived. It becomes a place that visitors enjoy because the space feels like home."

A custom wooden dining table from Etsy is surrounded by Drop chairs by Arne Jacobsen that were purchased from Design Within Reach. They are Brennen's favorite because they are at once sculpturally elegant and functional. The Random Light, by Bertjan Pot for Moooi and also from DWR, echoes the black below and adds weight and interest.

FROM: Queens, New York

LOCATED IN: Brooklyn, New York

INFLUENCES: Eileen Gray, Alexander McQueen, Henrik Vibskov, Kelly Wearstler, Vicente Wolf, Sheila Bridges, Arne Jacobsen, Charlotte Perriand—the list can go on for miles. They are creators who have their own styles, and that is why their work is classic and stands the test of time.

THE LOOK: Urban, sophisticated, graphic, and comfortable.

COLOR: I think every room needs a bit of black. It warms up a space, adds contrast and drama, and gives an airy room some heft. I believe contrast is the ultimate color scheme because it is the yin and yang that create balance. I do appreciate color, but in smaller doses. I don't do color for the sake of color.

KEY ELEMENT: Great art, no matter the price point. Art makes a space personal. It communicates history and dreams. It can be serious or playful. And I don't see art as just paintings on a wall—art can be collections of objects or a piece of beautifully displayed heirloom furniture.

ALWAYS HAVE: Flowers! They make a room come to life. For me, less is more when it comes to accessories, but there's always room for flowers.

INSPIRATION: Travel gets my brain flowing. I prefer places where people use what they have and waste very little.

NEVER FORGET: Listening as well as patience are the key to designing a space. When the designer and owner listen, the end result is a place that feels good to be in, that feels right.

OPPOSITE: The chairs are vintage T chairs in black leather with chrome frames designed by William Katavolos in collaboration with Douglas Kelley and Ross Littell; they were a gift from the homeowner's father. The velvet pillows provide a layer of subdued color in the otherwise neutral living room. The art ledge features the client's vintage prints and family photos and is off-center so it does not dominate the space.

TOP: This baker's cabinet was stripped back to stainless steel and embodies the client's love of all things vintage and modern. The piece also affords a creative way to organize and display collections. (left) The brass-and-glass bar cart gets the festivities started: it houses a vintage record player, records, and liquor for drinks. The glass vase on top adds a sculptural element. (right)

BOTTOM: The idea here was to keep the bedroom light and airy. The large-scale canvas acts as a feature and brings the eye up. The velvet pillows add color and texture, while the pair of Clam floor lamps from MoMA, though made of steel and marble, appear delicate.

"The best rooms are long on style and short on pretense. They are the kinds of rooms that invite the visitor to enjoy the business of living."

LILLY BUNN

Lilly Bunn began her career as an editor in the fashion department of *Town & Country* magazine before joining the venerable interiors firm McMillen Inc. So it's easy to understand how her rooms effortlessly incorporate contemporary style with traditional elements. Priding herself on providing the finest furnishings and finishes on every project, Bunn personally works with decorative artisans throughout the New York area and is always searching for the next great resource. This hands-on attention to detail has garnered her a steadfast client base, especially young families. Not one to shy away from strong color or distinct patterns, Bunn creates rooms that are fun, cheerful, and well edited.

One of Bunn's important tenets is that a well-designed room should be comfortable and accessible. She explains, "My work focuses on the collaboration with my clients. I'm interested in creating rooms that my clients feel at home in, not rooms meant to be seen as grand or pretentious."

A graphic Cole & Son wallpaper in teal and bronze is an unconventional choice for this stylish New York City library. A chocolate-brown sofa and a teal Parsons table echo the colors of the walls, which are also reflected in the brass-and-glass end table.

FROM: New York, New York

LOCATED IN: New York, New York

INFLUENCES: Sister Parish, of course, together with Albert Hadley. Their firm Parish-Hadley was a training ground for dozens of now-acclaimed decorators. Like some of my peers, I spend most of my days trying to live up to—and put a twist on—their traditional American decorating.

THE LOOK: Casual, fashionable, and cool.

COLOR: I think about color in decorating the same way I think about dressing myself in the morning: What is fashionable, comfortable, and necessary to accomplish this look?

KEY ELEMENT: A *very* deep sofa with lots of pillows that fits the entire family, especially when there's a TV in the room. You'll spend a great deal of time sitting on your sofa, so comfort is paramount.

ALWAYS HAVE: Juxtaposition. In color, as in strong hues mixed with neutrals. In textures, as in shiny against rough, metal against wood, nubby against smooth. And I love framed pictures. I know people want less stuff hanging around on tables, but pictures of family members, trips, or good friends help personalize a room.

INSPIRATION: New York has always been my inspiration! The energy and the optimism fuel every single place—and thing—that I design. Anything can happen in New York. I want my spaces to reflect that feeling of hope and excitement.

NEVER FORGET: Detailed, well-executed craftsmanship elevates what might otherwise be mundane to the artistic; it's what gives furnishings personality. An average chair, for example, is elevated with interesting lines and quiet dressmaker details. Great design makes ordinary things look beautiful.

OPPOSITE: A table from Organic Modernism takes center stage in this dining area, and doubles as a play table for the children of this young family. A custom-made red banquette adds sophistication for the occasional dinner party.

ABOVE: A large-scale Lucite coffee table keeps the open sensibility of this light-filled family room. Shots of color abound in a green midcentury club chair, a coral-hued carpet, and a raspberry throw. The sofa cushions have been made family-friendly so you can flip them in case of a spill.

RIGHT: World-map wallpaper enlivens a boy's room.

"I like to use beautiful mirrors interchangeably with art to punctuate a vignette— everything from a crusty, antique gilded mirror to small round convex mirrors."

PALOMA CONTRERAS

Best-selling author Paloma Contreras traveled an unorthodox path to a career in interior design, having graduated from the University of Houston with a degree in Spanish and Italian studies. From there, she taught advanced placement Spanish at a high school; she enjoyed the work, but she found herself craving more creative fulfillment.

In 2007, Contreras and her husband, Fabian, purchased their first home and set about decorating it. She remembers searching for decorating inspiration online and not finding much, so she began to write about the type of design that she found inspiring on her now famous blog, *La Dolce Vita*. After a year building an audience and being featured in a couple of shelter magazines, Contreras started getting offers for design jobs, so she left teaching to pursue design full-time. In 2013 she took a big leap and started her firm, Paloma Contreras Design. Her first monograph, *Dream Design Live*, was published in 2018.

modern-day designers such as Veere Grenney, Daniel Romualdez, Jacques Grange, and Michele Bönan, all of whom have an innate ability to switch effortlessly between styles without being pigeonholed into one specific look.

THE LOOK: A modern take on traditional style.

COLOR: I love color and find that it is most powerful when used sparingly. Having a neutral foundation allows accent colors to be the heroes of the space.

KEY ELEMENTS: On a fundamental note, every room needs symmetry and good scale for balance. In terms of more stylistic design elements, every room can benefit from good lighting and a hint of luxurious velvet.

ALWAYS HAVE: Hand-painted chinoiserie wallpaper; Louis XVI dining chairs; handsome, antique French commodes; rich velvet; and beautiful mirrors. Because these elements are more traditional, I like to pair them with abstract art, graphic ikat textiles, clean-lined upholstery, and modern lighting. The juxtaposition creates a wonderful tension.

INSPIRATION: While it sounds terribly cliché, I have fallen in love with Paris in the last few years. I have

FROM: Houston, Texas

LOCATED IN: Houston, Texas

INFLUENCES: I would say the work of Billy Baldwin, William Haines, David Hicks, and Albert Hadley continues to resonate deeply with me. I believe the greatest commonality among them is the way in which they would mix both traditional and modern elements so they felt completely fresh, yet undoubtedly timeless—something that I strive to achieve in each of the spaces I design. I am also inspired by

In this foyer, a vignette was created that plays up the designer's love of symmetry. The abstract painting is by Erin McIntosh from Gregg Irby Gallery. A Bunny Williams lamp sits atop a French commode, and Louis XVI–style chairs in a pale blue-gray velvet are placed under a pair of convex mirrors.

become obsessed with shopping for French antiques and vintage items. I always visit the Musée Picasso, the Musée Rodin, and the Musée des Arts Décoratifs. Not only is each of the buildings beautiful, but the works within them are also incredibly inspiring. Pablo Picasso is among my favorite artists, and he was such a brilliant marketer. It's fascinating to see the way Auguste Rodin lived, and the Musée des Arts Décoratifs is an absolute must for any design lover.

NEVER FORGET: Don't be overwhelmed by the process. The best rooms are layered and personal and can take a while to come together the way they are meant to. It's okay to hold out until you find the perfect piece.

OPPOSITE: The focal point of the dining room is the beautiful Madame de Pompadour wallpaper by Miles Redd for Schumacher. The skirted host and hostess chairs are mixed with carved-plinth side chairs; the combination lends a bit of casual flair to an otherwise traditional space.

TOP: The oversize formal living room, with its soaring windows, presented a challenge: finding a way to make it comfortable and cozy. To manage the task, two distinct seating areas were created that center around a custom double-sided sofa.

CENTER: In this corner of the dining room, a custom settee covered in Brunschwig & Fils's Bromo velvet and a Lucite drinks table add a touch of modern style. (left) This expansive space required large-scale furnishings to ground it. Grouping a grid of framed intaglios above a custom banquette created a focal point. (right)

BOTTOM: Abundant sunlight and feminine details define this master bedroom. The chinoiserie panels flanking the bed were custom painted for the space.

WILL COOPER

New York–based designer Will Cooper, partner and Chief Creative Officer of the multidisciplinary firm ASH NYC, has always felt design was an innate part of his character. Even as a young child, he had a fascination with arranging and rearranging his room. He was enthralled by an aunt's design business in Washington. "She would import huge containers of European antiques, and I thought it was the most exciting thing," he says. "I remember visiting her homes and spaces and thinking that she had hung the moon."

In the summer of 2007, Cooper arrived in New York City for an internship at Ralph Lauren, and in short order he joined the staff. It was there that he learned the ropes of retail design and worked with some of the most talented people in the world. Cooper eventually met fellow ASH partners Ari Heckman and Jonathan Minkoff through mutual friends, and the three combined forces to launch the firm in 2011. In the beginning, ASH focused on real estate development and staging for real estate. However, staging quickly blossomed into doing permanent design work for interiors ranging from hospitality to residential.

among those published by Paige Rense at *Architectural Digest*; Maison Jansen, whose breadth of work is nothing short of astounding; and Michael Taylor, a standout of the 1980s decorators.

THE LOOK: Always changing, as influenced by the architecture, the geolocation, and, of course, the client.

COLOR: I used to be scared of color, and there was a time in design when it felt taboo. As I've matured and opened my eyes to the past, I've realized that color is an integral part of every interior. I love color now. I have developed a palette of specific hues of red, blue, yellow, and green that I always try to weave into my interiors.

KEY ELEMENT: Antique and vintage pieces that ground each room with their narrative and soul. I love discovering provenance and sharing that story with a client—there is something so much more appealing about living with pieces that have a backstory, and being a steward that carries the torch for such pieces is what makes a house a home.

ALWAYS HAVE: Books—they tell the story of the person occupying the room. Plants also give a room life and oxygen. I like playing with scale. In a hotel lobby, for example, the palms can be fourteen or fifteen feet high, and they add such a dramatic element to a room that makes it feel finished.

INSPIRATION: Traveling to Belgium in 2012 was revolutionary for me. I

FROM: Fort Worth, Texas

LOCATED IN: New York, New York

INFLUENCES: I look to historical designers for inspiration. Some of my favorites are Piero Pinto, whose style cannot be pinned to one era; Angelo Donghia, who created a robust design firm and furniture empire; Renzo Mongiardino, whose risk-taking work spanned from exquisitely appointed castles to stark, modern interiors; Andrée Putman, whose look was so graphic and iconic; Sally Sirkin Lewis, a hidden gem

A pair of floor lamps by Paul Mayen flanking the entrance to the dining room in this New York City apartment cast an amber glow. The chairs have been casually draped in two-toned slipcovers. The dramatic artwork on the wall is by Iván Argote.

received a list of places to see and an introduction to Axel Vervoordt. Touring Vervoordt's office and home was a real turning point in terms of understanding the design world. His design influences from Japan were palpable in the spaces, and he is a maestro of creating a look that is unique to him.

NEVER FORGET: When designing someone's home, it's important to do a deep dive into how the person plans to use the space. What is his or her daily life like? Does he or she entertain? Read? Are there children or pets? I think it's paramount to design in a way that prepares for and accommodates these experiences.

TOP: A Gio Ponti desk from the 1950s is paired with a Vittorio Nobili chair from the same period in this corner of the sitting room. The hanging photograph is by David LaChapelle, and the leaning framed drawing is by Camille-Félix Bellanger.

BOTTOM: A custom mirror designed by Cooper for ASH NYC hangs in this master bathroom, which is clad in Carrara marble. Framed artworks on the vanity soften and add interest to the space.

OPPOSITE: A semicircular sofa designed in the 1970s by Kwok Hoï Chan for Steiner Paris dominates this sophisticated sitting room. The traditional architectural elements counterbalance and complement the mid- to late-twentieth-century furnishings. The bust on the mantel is by Salvador Dalí.

> *"I believe that design is invariably woven into culture; when I travel, I love to observe the complex interaction of the two in ways that are unique to each part of the world."*

KATI CURTIS

A former dancer, Kati Curtis has always been captivated by the human form. At first, her focus was on the grace and strength that dancers displayed. Later, a figure-drawing class at the Savannah College of Art and Design solidified her nascent design philosophy: that understating how the human form interacts with a space is crucial to its design.

Early in her design career, Curtis spent twelve years working at both architectural and engineering firms. This path was pivotal to her developing the ability to articulate her vision through drawings. Sketching and detailing are vital parts of her creative process; they make ideas much more accessible to coworkers and clients, a critical step in turning original visions into reality. And those visions are exciting: sophisticated color palettes, drawn from fine art or historical design and architecture, imbue beautifully proportioned and classically detailed spaces, resulting in rooms that are as familiar as they are fresh.

I also feel a special attachment to the Jardin Majorelle, Yves Saint Laurent's picturesque villa in Marrakech, with its breathtaking scale and variety.

THE LOOK: Sophisticated, classical, colorful.

COLOR: I have great admiration for architect Robert Adam, for his classical order, his seemingly perfect use of proportion, and, most compellingly, his use of color. I have some of his elevation images hanging in my office, and any one of them could be used as color-palette inspiration for our contemporary projects. His peachy and strawberry pinks, his mint greens and beautiful teals, and his Wedgwood blues all still resonate deeply with my creative sensibility.

KEY ELEMENT: Indigenous textiles, because they are works of art. In Bali, Indonesia, I watched artists weaving an ikat fabric in a pattern that specifically represented the life of their village. Seeing how meticulous they were in their craft, how proud they were to represent their cultural symbols in their work, is an experience that has deep meaning for me to this day. I've had similar moments in India, where I watched artisans hand-blocking the most beautiful, unique fabrics, and Morocco, where I observed the most luxurious rugs being meticulously woven by hand.

When the homeowner moved from the Upper East Side to the Upper West Side of Manhattan, she wanted a more casual look. Grass-cloth wallpaper strikes the right rustic note. The Art Deco sofa, designed in the 1940s by James Mont, was purchased at Todd Merrill in New York and reupholstered in a navy silk velvet. Graphic black-and-white prints and pillows composed of the client's own needlework complete the unstudied look.

FROM: Portland, Maine

LOCATED IN: New York, New York and Los Angeles, California

INFLUENCES: I am influenced by many of the designers who have come before me. I am awed by Sister Parish's ability to mix different styles into one unified whole and by Tony Duquette's remarkable Los Angeles home, Dawnridge. Duquette's ability to incorporate the many disparate elements from his travels across the globe is something I strive to emulate.

50

ALWAYS HAVE: For me, there are three essential things for a successful room: a vintage rug, as it adds color and style and anchors a room with history; at least one piece of furniture that has a story attached to it; and art that has some kind of meaning to its owner.

INSPIRATION: When I travel, I am exposed to creative landscapes so vastly different from my own that I am forced to continually reevaluate and update my perspective. Each of these encounters has had a lasting impact on my creative process, and they continue to inform and complement my design aesthetic.

NEVER FORGET: If design is, in fact, a continuum, then it is always moving forward. While we embrace the history of what came before us, we must also welcome those changes in technology and process that help us move the medium into the future. To that end, computers, software, and new-media platforms have a crucial part to play in turning one's design vision into reality.

OPPOSITE: Hand-painted in China, this classic chinoiserie wallpaper from Fromental sheathes the bedroom walls in a playful aviary.

TOP: Archival prints from Karen Tompkins's Arctic series—the artist is a friend of the homeowner—balance the warmth of the red grass-cloth walls. The custom headboard is covered in a Carolina Irving Textiles linen.

BOTTOM: For this windowless entry, Curtis gold-leafed the ceiling and faux-painted the walls with metallic flecks to reflect ambient light. The demilune table is an eighteenth-century antique purchased in Hudson, New York. (left) The library is just off the entryway, so the gold-leafed ceiling extends into this space as well. Custom bookshelves create a niche where a tufted banquette covered in moss velvet masters two tasks: providing seating above and storage underneath. (right)

*"Try something new. Taking risks is
what a life in design is all about."*

ASHLEY DARRYL

Nuanced is the adjective you think of when seeing a room designed by New York City–based Ashley Darryl—a subtle monochromatic space that, upon careful consideration, reveals richly textured layers. Floor coverings are painterly and abstract or graphically geometric, providing a shot of drama underfoot. Understated walls recede to offer the perfect calming antidote to twenty-first-century life, while metallic finishes and contemporary artwork inflect Darryl's rooms with glamour.

Originally from Texas, Darryl grew up antiquing with her mother, who is also an interior designer. She moved to New York for graduate school at Sotheby's Institute of Art and opened her own firm in 2014 after a stint working for Jeff Lincoln.

FROM: Tyler, Texas

LOCATED IN: New York, New York

INFLUENCES: Billy Baldwin for his clean-lined furnishings, Jean-Michel Frank for his masterful layering, Jacques Grange for rich nuance, and David Hicks for pattern and geometry.

THE LOOK: Understatement and comfort—layered yet minimal.

COLOR: My thesis paper in college was on Pompeii, and the palette of the frescoes continues to influence me to this day. What were once vibrant turquoise, red, and emerald green have been dulled by time and weather to dusty blue, rose, and mint green, with only bits of bright color still intact. To recreate this feel, I turn to the Farrow & Ball hues Parma Gray, Setting Plaster, and Pink Ground,

Three signed and framed lithographs by Joan Miró hang above a richly tufted sofa in this New York City living room. The serene color scheme of the furnishings and carpet allow the artwork to remain the focus, while the fireplace adds visual warmth year-round.

keeping the colors neutral and soft with the occasional bright splash here and there. My go-to white paint is Benjamin Moore's Paper White. It has a bit of a gray tint to it versus other whites that can go blue or yellow.

KEY ELEMENT: It is pivotal to have a special piece in each room, such as a newly upholstered vintage chair, a unique accessory from the flea market, or something custom made.

ALWAYS HAVE: Greenery. Whether it's a tree in a large glazed pot or a small sprout on a windowsill, it will add life to the space. I love ficus trees and ferns. Their organic shapes soften hard furniture lines.

INSPIRATION: Colors on a building, architectural elements on a house, landscapes, a cool old door—I photograph all sorts of things for my files.

NEVER FORGET: Functionality! Everyone wants a beautiful space to live in, but how do we make it functional without jeopardizing the beauty? I am always striving to make spaces not only beautiful but also livable for modern young families.

OPPOSITE: The natural texture of the rivet-patterned wallpaper gives this foyer flair, while the sophisticated tableau sets the stage for what's to come in the rest of the home.

TOP: In the master bedroom, the striped curtains were added to bring color and playfulness into the space.

CENTER: One of the mandates from the client was to create a blue room, and the dining room proved the perfect place to make a statement. An original Salvador Dalí hangs above the fireplace.

BOTTOM: A fresh white kitchen features jewellike brass-and–milk glass pendants above the island.

> *"For a truly harmonious interior, the architecture of the space should dictate the scale, proportion, and mood of the furnishings and materials."*

KEVIN DUMAIS

Kevin Dumais grew up in a hardworking middle-class family. His parents took pride in their house, and his sister inspired him with her creativity. The family home was a place of strong family values, close friends, and an open-door policy. "This might be why I am so connected with the world of residential design, because I love the idea of home," Dumais says. "Each new client I work with allows me to interpret his or her idea of home and cultivate an approach that reflects his or her values."

Taking the knowledge he gleaned in the interiors program at the New England School of Art & Design at Suffolk University, Dumais began his career with a small Boston design firm. This was followed by a stint at a furniture-design firm and then as a senior designer at S. Russell Groves in New York. From there, Dumais was well prepared to open his own firm.

Dumais's rooms are restrained, but with a sense of casual luxury: richly layered with a mix of midcentury pieces, subdued palettes, and contemporary art. In his own words, he tries "to balance grace with comfort so the spaces feel effortless and well suited to a modern lifestyle."

COLOR: I have fond memories of spending summer weekends on the beaches of New Hampshire and Maine. I find colors that are drawn from this coastal New England environment very comforting; they make me feel at home. The foundation of my palette is often warm, neutral grays and sandy, putty tones that feel fresh when paired with crisp blacks and whites; rich, earthy colors; and blues found in the ocean.

KEY ELEMENT: Midcentury furniture. What I really like about the midcentury aesthetic are the clean, fluid lines, refined proportions, and simple approachability to the furniture.

ALWAYS HAVE: Blues in various shades and tones and neutrals in various textures; prominent light fixtures, pottery, hair-on hides, textured oak and walnut finishes; and tranquil bedrooms.

INSPIRATION: I love trips to the ocean, in particular Provincetown, Massachusetts, where I am recharged and inspired by the quaint Colonial and Federal architecture. I absolutely love Paris, as well as the South of France. The local flea market in Nice is a treasure, and the city of Èze is breathtaking. Oh, and Bali: My husband and I went there for our honeymoon; it inspired my use of batik textiles in my work.

NEVER FORGET: Interior architecture and decoration have a big impact on each other—it cannot be underestimated.

The classic Floating Curved sofa by Vladimir Kagan is upholstered in velvet; the curvature of the clean, modern lines keeps this central seating group opposite the kitchen feeling light and connects one area to the other. The chain-link floor lamp was found at a flea market, refurbished, and finished with a custom overscale burlap shade with leather trim.

FROM: Lorain, Ohio

LOCATED IN: New York, New York

INFLUENCES: I love the design and craftsmanship of twentieth-century furnishings and Scandinavian design, pieces by such luminaries as Edward Wormley, Børge Mogensen, Kaare Klint, Hans Wegner, Jean-Michel Frank, Carl Auböck, John Dickinson, Marcel Breuer, Jean Prouvé, Milo Baughman, and T. H. Robsjohn-Gibbings.

THE LOOK: Tailored, calm, edited.

OPPOSITE: To allow southern light to filter into the master suite, we designed a steel-and–reeded glass partition as a nod to the building's past as a warehouse. A midcentury lounge chair was re-covered in a windowpane wool felt and leather.

ABOVE: In the kitchen, Farrow & Ball's Hague Blue appears on the millwork. The extra-large island is balanced with an original half-barrel pendant covered in linen, which provides a soft ambient glow.

RIGHT: A custom wood console table was inspired by a 1930s table by Axel Einar Hjorth, and it's topped with a stoneware lamp by Dumais Made. A Grecian urn, a nod to the clients' heritage, is tucked in the corner. (left) The intimate study, painted in Benjamin Moore's Amherst Gray, is maximized with a floating shelf and built-in desk. (right)

ERICK ESPINOZA

A first-generation American born and raised in Miami, Erick Espinoza has long been driven by his yearning for knowledge and advancement. His interest in design began in his youth with drawing and painting; for many years, he thought his calling was to be an artist. In high school, Espinoza interned with both a renowned residential architect and an international commercial architecture firm. For college, he was thrilled to be offered the Albert Hadley Scholarship to the New York School of Interior Design.

A longtime fan of Anthony Baratta and William Diamond's firm, Espinoza set his sights on joining their team and succeeded. Seven years later, he has climbed the ladder to become the creative director of Baratta's firm. In that capacity, he carries on the legacy of incorporating strong color, distinct and often demonstrative patterns, and a sense of wit into uniquely American spaces.

In this living room, it's all about the rug, inspired by one designed by Christian Bérard for Nelson A. Rockefeller. The furnishings were kept light and neutral with curvaceous lines, and they include a Deco chair from Argentina, a custom credenza, and an arch-topped mirror from the 1970s modeled after Jean-Michel Frank. A Chinese ancestral artwork is hung behind the chair.

FROM: Miami, Florida

LOCATED IN: New York, New York

INFLUENCES: Billy Baldwin, Albert Hadley, Michael Taylor, Robert Adam, Sister Parish, David Hicks, Jean-Michel Frank, Émile-Jacques Ruhlmann, and Renzo Mongiardino. There is so much to learn from looking at the work of these designers: the architectural components and tricks to making a room work; the mix of unexpected colors and patterns; and the different takes on tradition and classicism. And of course, I'm influenced by Anthony Baratta, who taught me to study the best of the best.

THE LOOK: Colorful, layered, and pattern-centric.

COLOR: Color is a must in my work. The way that I disperse color is very methodical, and I make a conscious effort to spread it throughout a room or entire residence. I look to Henri Matisse for inspiration.

KEY ELEMENT: Pattern. There's a rhythm and dance to the successful use of pattern; it has to feel somewhat familiar, yet fresh at the same time.

ALWAYS HAVE: Color! And an understanding of a room's natural light. The more natural daylight a room has, the more you can play around with hues and values of color. If a room lacks sunlight, you can either do a pale color on the walls to brighten it, or you can embrace the darkness and go with a deep or rich color.

INSPIRATION: I consider myself lucky to be part of a generation with so much inspiration at our fingertips. I have a fever for research: I love my books and old magazines dearly and look at them often, but the Internet has opened up so many avenues to study the past for inspiration. Even images from books that are no longer in print can be found online with the right dedication.

NEVER FORGET: The best thing you can do is empty a room of all the tchotchkes, trinkets, artwork, and family portraits and start with a clean slate. With an editor's eye, put back only what is essential and most representative of you and your personal style. The rest can be reconsidered for another space.

OPPOSITE: A curved sofa was reupholstered in a subtle chenille fabric from Osborne & Little and hugs graphic Matisse-inspired pillows. The sofa invites you to come sit and relax, while touches of red create high contrast.

ABOVE: In a bedroom, the variations in scale make the eye dance around the room. The streamlined chair adds a modern feeling—like a Jackie O. coat—and mimics the clean lines of the bed it faces. The antique Irish pine armoire further accentuates the height of the room. (left) An unexpected, overscale houndstooth is a classic that packs a punch in this bedroom, where the red trimming unifies the apartment's theme. The Chinese ancestral painting was hung high to give the room a sense of height. Antiques add a sense of history when mixed with newer pieces. (right)

> *"Visit flea markets, shops, both modest and grand, and auction houses. This is how to learn different ways of making, and different ways of seeing."*

CHARLIE FERRER

There's clear evidence that disciplined restraint drives New York interior and furnishings designer Charlie Ferrer; his rooms feel as if nothing needs to be removed and nothing needs to be added. The balance is equally studied and effortless—not an easy feat.

Having started his career in Los Angeles working with architect Sarah Jensen and interior designer Timothy Corrigan, Ferrer leaped into furniture design and launched MEIER/FERRER, a Los Angeles–based furniture and design gallery that sold tailored modern pieces alongside other contemporary work, vintage pieces, and art. After a three-year run, he shifted gears again by moving to New York and setting up an interior design practice, FERRER, in the Flatiron District.

FROM: Greenwich, Connecticut

LOCATED IN: New York, New York and London, England.

INFLUENCES: My work is strongest when I touch all aspects of the design process. I favor fully integrated projects in which architecture, furniture and lighting, objects, and art support and inform one another. I am first an interior designer, second a dealer, and third an aspiring architect. I'm inspired by the work of architects who designed complete environments for which they created furniture, lighting, and fixtures—

Mixing new and old in this living room, Ferrer chose a Dmitriy & Co. sofa for its generous depth. Textural pillows add to its comfort. The sculptural midcentury Danish chair at right balances the silhouette of the French wicker chair at left that was purchased in Paris.

ABOVE: The headboard in this art-filled bedroom is actually a vintage Czechoslovakian room divider upholstered and repurposed for the space. (left) Three carved-wood sconces were linked into a single unit and wired with a twisted silk-covered cord that speaks to the vintage flair throughout. The wooden stool is by Jean Touret and the Artisans of Marolles. (right)

OPPOSITE: A striking photograph by Jill Greenberg dominates the wall space in what serves as a casual home office. The two buckets are actually works by Los Angeles–based artist Matthias Merkel Hess, who re-envisions seemingly mundane objects as ceramics.

multidisciplinary power talents like Luis Barragán, Angelo Mangiarotti, the Milanese collective BBPR, Gunnar Asplund, and Ettore Sottsass.

THE LOOK: Balanced eclecticism with a modern focus.

COLOR: Personally, I am comfortable with the absence of color. But I love using purples, blues, greens, and orange, too. I encourage clients to identify colors they respond to. Then I strive to create environments that are calming and comfortable around their preferences. In that way clients connect to their spaces on cerebral and visceral levels through color.

KEY ELEMENT: Fine art plays a critical role in my work. Just like with furniture and objects, in art, I believe a balanced mix is best. I like combining

works of different mediums and periods in my projects.

ALWAYS HAVE: Incredible vintage lighting. I love lighting that tells a story. The more funky and unique, the better.

INSPIRATION: Visual artists of all stripes inspire: the painter Gerhard Richter, the photographer Wolfgang Tillmans, and the lesser-known but no less extraordinary sculptor Matthias Merkel Hess. I also find works by contemporary decorative artisans influential, including glassblower Andrew Hughes, furniture designer Erik Gustafson, and lighting designer Kacper Dolatowski.

NEVER FORGET: That quality lasts— quality of craftsmanship *and* quality of design. The timeless interior is grounded in quality.

DAN FINK

Dan Fink studied human biology at Stanford University, so it's safe to say he came to a career in interior design in an unexpected way. While at school, he found himself spending hours with his head in art books. Fink says, "I wanted to live a creative life, even if I didn't know it."

When he graduated, Fink was hired as an assistant to a prominent Silicon Valley entrepreneur, and one of his assignments was to plan retreats for his boss. "I would find the locations—far-flung and exotic—and plan all the logistics. Often the venues needed staging, and I found myself treating them as little design projects. I would borrow furniture from local antiques shops, spend early mornings in the flower markets, iron tablecloths well into the night—all with the aim of creating a magical setting for the guests." He did well enough that when his boss needed an interior designer, Fink was given the chance. Soon, other prominent figures in the tech world hired Fink as well, and he had an interior-design business almost overnight.

THE LOOK: Finely tailored interiors with a modern elegance and timeless ease.

COLOR: I look at color and pattern very practically, almost scientifically; how to excite the eye isn't magic, it's careful consideration. It's about relationships between two or more things—cool and warm colors, large and small scale, composition, order.

KEY ELEMENT: Balance. Whether traditional or modern, layered or minimalist, colorful or monotone, the best rooms find peace among a mix of complementary and often contrasting elements.

ALWAYS HAVE: I look to a mix of objects—ancient and modern, rustic and fine—and, of course, lots of inspiring books.

INSPIRATION: I'm inspired by the juxtaposition of different cultures and periods—midcentury and Deco, Japanese and English, California cool and old New York—and materials, such as rough and fine together and industrial with fancy.

NEVER FORGET: Remember that the homes we make tell stories about us. They're the settings of life's great moments and the quiet backdrop and listener to every laugh and bedtime prayer.

FROM: Franklin Lakes, New Jersey

LOCATED IN: New York, New York and Bellport, New York

INFLUENCES: Sir John Soane, for his perfect, classical detailing of modern buildings of the time. Jean-Michel Frank, because his interiors and furnishings are simplicity and finery at their best. Eileen Gray, as she represents the intersection of art, intellect, and luxury. Charles and Ray Eames, for always having fun.

In the entry hall of this San Francisco home, Pablo Picasso's *Jacqueline au Bandeau* takes pride of place above an elegantly curved settee designed by Andrée Putman. The wallpaper is Tobacco Silhouette by Gracie.

OPPOSITE: A remarkable nineteenth-century Japanese screen was framed for the room and continues the gold color scheme into the dining room. Sophisticated yet sedate, the carved painted chairs and a chandelier by Thomas O'Brien allow the screen to be the focal point.

TOP: A tranquil Hiroshi Sugimoto seascape photograph sets the tone for this peaceful living room. Shades of brown, cream, and caramel punctuate the room.

RIGHT: In the master bedroom, Ansel Adams's *Moon and Half Dome* hangs above the custom upholstered bed. The 1930s side table is by Axel Einar Hjorth.

OLIVER M. FURTH

It's no surprise that a boy who asked for a subscription to *Architectural Digest* for his ninth birthday went on to a career in interior design, and this is exactly what happened with fourth-generation Angeleno Oliver M. Furth. His career started when a family friend invited Furth to work at her interior design office after school. Then at age sixteen, he landed an entry-level position at the architecture firm of Marc Appleton, where he ran errands, made copies, and organized samples. "I loved being around the creativity in Marc's office," Furth says. "I learned a tremendous amount about the design business."

Before opening his eponymous design firm in 2004, Furth trained under some of the best: Martyn Lawrence Bullard, Michael S. Smith, Trip Haenisch, and the late Greg Jordan. In addition to his design practice, Furth runs an experimental design gallery, Furth Yashar &. He also consults for the Los Angeles County Museum of Art, where he is chair emeritus of LACMA's Decorative Arts and Design Council—the youngest person ever to hold this prestigious position.

FROM: Los Angeles, California

LOCATED IN: Los Angeles, California

INFLUENCES: Many of Jean-Michel Frank's concepts, like square-arm sofas, forever changed the face of modern design. Michael Taylor capitalized on the California look and reinvented American decorating, playing high and low against each other brilliantly well before this was the norm. I also admire Milton Glaser, the graphic designer famous for the "I ♥ NY" campaign, who speaks about finding the right balance of foreign and familiar—giving an audience something they know and also something they don't know. I often apply this to my own work, finding the right balance of proven ideas that people are comfortable with while also pushing the dialogue forward.

THE LOOK: Layered modernism.

COLOR: Color is an incredibly important ingredient when putting a room together, and it can be the single most impactful element of a space. I prefer to use color judiciously, keeping in mind the existing conditions: how much light enters the space and where; the style; the architecture; historical color palettes; the client's personality; and how much emphasis we want on the objects or artwork in a room.

KEY ELEMENT: A rich mix of materials. Harry Winston revolutionized contemporary American jewelry design in the middle of the twentieth century, designing baubles with simple settings intended to highlight the stones. "Materials first" is a theory you can successfully apply to many disciplines, from cooking to architecture to interior design.

ALWAYS HAVE: Books, fresh flowers, and something a visitor or houseguest might pick up to use or enjoy.

A large canvas by contemporary artist Alex Israel establishes a dialogue with the organic shape of the coffee table by Wendell Castle in this living room. The metallic-leaf ceiling further amplifies the abundant sunlight in the space, and the custom rug is by the Rug Company.

INSPIRATION: There's so much inspiration out there! As a curious person, one simply needs to open his or her eyes to find stimulus. The way warm and cool greens mix together in nature could become a palette for a room, the ruffled edge of a Giambattista Valli dress could inform a curtain detail, or a nineteenth-century African fetish sculpture could be reinterpreted in a wall texture.

NEVER FORGET: A well-designed home needs to express a feeling of context: where it is in the world and who lives there.

TOP: Another view of the living room reveals a beautiful arched window framed by curtains that repeat throughout the room. A pair of slipper chairs and a pair of armchairs add symmetry.

CENTER: A wood-clad ceiling, complete with exposed beams, sets a more casual vibe for the family room. Deep upholstered sofas and chairs provide an opportunity for friends to gather and converse. The vintage coffee table is by Karl Springer.

BOTTOM: A custom silver leaf–and-leather bed designed by Furth, a bronze ceiling fixture, a bronze-and-travertine side table, rock-crystal sconces, and a vintage mirrored stool mingle to telegraph refined glamour in this master bedroom.

OPPOSITE: The light refracting from a Baccarat chandelier sets the tone for this high-style dining room. A macassar ebony table, designed by Furth, is paired with vintage German chairs from the 1930s.

JOSHUA GREENE

Born in Southern California, a few blocks from the beach, New York-based designer Joshua Greene traces his interest in design to the architecture of L.A.'s grand homes from another era, specifically those in the town of San Marino, where he attended elementary school. His mother had a small design business when he was young, which, along with countless hours constructing elaborate Lego houses with long driveways (he still loves a grand approach to a house), seeded his interest in décor. When Greene was in middle school, the family moved to Seattle, where Greene was exposed to the Pacific Northwest and its influences: the natural world, its indigenous people, and Japan.

After a stint covering fashion for *WWD* and a position at MR Architecture + Decor, Greene landed at what he calls "the best finishing school in Manhattan": Ralph Lauren. He traveled the world opening stores, the zenith of which was launching the flagship store on Boulevard Saint-Germain in Paris. During that time, he started taking on small freelance interior design jobs. He went to work for Michael S. Smith in Los Angeles, eventually returning to New York City to establish the interior design department at Sawyer | Berson, which he ran for several years. He founded Josh Greene Design in 2018.

Clean-lined geometry was the inspiration for this Brooklyn townhouse, and it shows up in the oversize mirror from John Salibello, the throw pillows on the sofa, and the lower shelf of the coffee table. The chandelier, from Ralph Lauren Home, has a Bauhaus sensibility that the client, from Vienna, appreciates.

FROM: La Jolla, California

LOCATED IN: New York, New York

INFLUENCES: The great residential architects like David Adler, and especially those from Southern California, such as Wallace Neff and Paul Williams, are major influences for me. Also Frank Lloyd Wright. Palm Springs was always a family destination. The midcentury architects, like Richard Neutra, Donald Wexler, William Cody, and Paul Rudolph, are also huge influences.

THE LOOK: Comfortable, logical spaces, with strict attention paid to scale and proportion.

COLOR: I like colors that feel as if they've been left out in the sun for a bit. Maybe it's my California youth. I tend to steer clear of punchy primaries, but that doesn't mean I don't do color. I just don't want color to be jarring. I like odd colors and soft colors.

KEY ELEMENT: A mix of furniture from various time periods. Every room I design has this juxtaposition, but there is no formula to it. It could be a midcentury cabinet with a Georgian mirror above it or a postmodern side table next to a custom-designed sofa. Pieces from different periods have different materials, different weights, and different lines, but if they're all beautiful and speak to one another, then you've got an interesting space.

ALWAYS HAVE: Large-scale art. A room can't "sing" without it.

INSPIRATION: I think because of my 1980s California and Palm Springs roots, Michael Taylor has always been someone to whom I look for inspiration. I love his overscale upholstery in sumptuous fabrics and bulbous shapes. There is a comfort there that I have always liked. His designs are stylish, but they also have a relationship to their surroundings and

the outdoors. They're easy to live in. For 1970s glam, I love David Hicks and Angelo Donghia.

NEVER FORGET: There has to be a reason behind the design decisions you make, and you need to be able to explain that clearly to your clients. Sharing your thought process is important; it can help persuade a client to get on board with something he or she might not be comfortable with. In the end, design is about communication.

TOP: With such high ceilings, the large artwork by Jen Wink Hays, hanging above a faux-malachite console by Karl Springer, feels perfectly scaled in the dining room. The chairbacks carry the geometric theme into the space. (left) In the guest bedroom, a midcentury Italian chair and ottoman upholstered in a ZAK+FOX fabric welcome the visitor to relax in a corner flooded with natural light. The painting is by Katie DeGroot. (right)

BOTTOM: The masculine yet comfortable master bedroom is anchored by a midcentury Swedish rug, which the client fell in love with. The ceiling is painted the faintest shade of blue to introduce color to the otherwise neutral space.

OPPOSITE: In the earthy library, linear patterns, drawn from the striped kilim, abound. The vintage chairs were purchased in great shape and fit the color scheme, so they were left as is.

*"Use color to infuse joyfulness
into your rooms."*

BRIA HAMMEL

Minnesota-based interior designer Bria Hammel credits her mother, who always had a keen interest in decorating, with sparking her interest in design. The pair often visited wallpaper stores and furniture galleries in Hammel's youth.

White is a constant in Hammel's work, from clear, pure shades to those inflected with the slightest touch of cream or a whisper of a cooler gray. But that's not to suggest Hammel's rooms lack color; to the contrary, color punctuates her spaces, often with a touch of feminine flair.

Hammel has always been drawn to warm, casual spaces infused with old-fashioned elegance. Understated architectural details, beautiful millwork, graphic elements, and supremely comfortable furnishings combine to set the stage for spaces that invite the visitor to come in, sit back, and join the conversation.

FROM: St. Paul, Minnesota

LOCATED IN: St. Paul, Minnesota

INFLUENCES: Sister Parish, for her love of the color pink and her skill with color and pattern. The casual elegance she brought to every space is exactly what I try to bring to my work. Her rooms still appear timeless.

THE LOOK: Clean, crisp, supremely comfortable.

COLOR: I use color to set a tone or mood in every space we design. I gravitate toward soft, calming colors, as those are the type of environments we strive to create. A color should always be paired with a contrasting hue. I design using cool and warm colors in every room. If

The arched windows and fireplace mantel were preserved in a renovation, then updated with a fresh color and marble surround. Antique candelabras sourced from Kansas City flank the Kayce Hughes artwork. Oversize Ralph Lauren Home table lamps create drama and balance the scale of the room.

blue is the primary color, I like to offset it with camel or pink—a warm color to ground the cool tones of the space.

KEY ELEMENTS: Generously proportioned, plush upholstery; rattan.

ALWAYS HAVE: A touch of femininity. There is something nurturing and livable about feminine details in a room, whether it's a color or a decorative trim.

INSPIRATION: Other designers. Suzanne Kasler's work is infused with timeless elegance and feminine detail. And Mark D. Sikes is a fellow lover of the color blue! What I love most about Mark is his courage to embrace pattern in a room. I've never seen so many different types of stripes in one room that work so well together.

NEVER FORGET: When we're picking a white, we're always paying attention to not only the other furnishing, but the other colors in the room. If there is a lot of direct sunlight, we pick a cooler white. Less sunlight calls for a warmer white.

TOP: Brown rattan counter stools add texture and warmth to the kitchen. (left) The blue plaid wallpaper dresses up this stylish mudroom; the cement tile in a soft sand color manages the task of hiding dirt while adding another playful pattern to the space. (right)

BOTTOM: Floor-to-ceiling millwork was added to the living room to create formality. The picture rail was a classic detail installed to give the home a more historic feel and to allow artwork to be moved easily.

OPPOSITE: Custom newel posts on the staircase add a bit of stately grandeur. In juxtaposition, simple iron spindles give a modern touch to the otherwise traditional design. The feminine striped bench softens the mood.

GEORGIA TAPERT HOWE

The summer before her senior year at Hamilton College, where she was studying art history, Georgia Tapert Howe landed an internship in the New York office of legendary designer David Easton. Upon graduation, Howe accepted a full-time position at the Pace Gallery, but then realized it wasn't for her. Remembering how much she enjoyed working with Easton, she reached out to him. She was hired, and her life in interior design began.

After working for another legend, Mica Ertegun, and for the maverick firm Haynes-Roberts, Howe opened her first home-accessories boutique in New York City in 2007. She then relocated to Los Angeles in 2011 and opened her eponymous interior design firm there.

As an avid traveler and observer, Howe believes that good design should not be constrained by set boundaries or rules. Her progressive design philosophy is reflected in the myriad styles and periods that influence her interiors.

THE LOOK: Tailored, colorful, relaxed.

COLOR: I use a lot of color in my work. I tend to have love affairs with colors, passionate but short-lived before I move on. In general, I always seem to come back to greens, and browns, and a richer color palette. Green is my mainstay—almost all shades—and I never tire of it. In my own house, I don't use much color; I need a break from it after using it so often in my work.

KEY ELEMENT: A great antique. Antiques have stories; they lend a room history.

ALWAYS HAVE: I don't think a room is complete without art, books, and flowers. And, of course, friends and family to enjoy the space!

INSPIRATION: Old interiors magazines. There's always something of interest that has stood the test of time. And my clients—how they want to live in the space and what they respond to.

NEVER FORGET: I always remind clients that a house is the sum of all its parts. Sometimes they want every piece of furniture or fabric to be a showstopper, but you need to know where to hold back. Not everything can sing, and all the elements must work together. I even have to remind myself of this at times.

With a decidedly graphic wallpaper, everything else needed to be fairly neutral in this stylish dining room. An antique farm table with midcentury chairs creates a dialogue with a custom rope-wrapped chandelier. The mirror is from Lucca Antiques, one of the designer's favorite places to shop in Los Angeles.

FROM: London, England

LOCATED IN: Los Angeles, California

INFLUENCES: I've had the chance to work for some of the greats, and I learned so much from all of them. But no one has influenced my work more than Mica Ertegun. Her ability to mix the traditional with the contemporary to create chic, comfortable, and timeless rooms is unparalleled. It was while working for her that I really zeroed in on what I love and found my own style, and I still look to her work for inspiration.

OPPOSITE: In this overscale master bath, a wet room was created to house the tub and shower. Black steel–framed doors were nixed once the bright, bold tiles were chosen. The white-framed windows all the way around the bathroom provide a view of the mountains on one side and the ocean on the other.

TOP: This living room is centered around an eleven-foot-long sofa, the inspiration for which was a much smaller vintage frame that was copied and expanded for the space. The client loves color, so the blue polka-dot upholstery set the tone for the rest of the room. Mixed textures and periods create a layered look.

CENTER: An avowed animal lover, the client requested something animal-inspired in the house. A guest bedroom provided the perfect opportunity: big cats frolic in the brush on the wallcovering.

BOTTOM: The client's architect widened the patio to accommodate a firepit that was designed for the space, for total indoor-outdoor California living in a classic Spanish house. The built-in banquette and a nearby custom outdoor kitchen—complete with a pizza oven—make it perfect for entertaining.

"Having furniture that wows the viewer is wonderful, but having a sofa you can lounge on is more important."

YOUNG HUH

Young Huh started her design career in 2003, leaving behind her original career as an attorney. She founded Young Huh Interior Design in New York City in 2007 and has since worked on residential and commercial projects around the country.

Growing up Korean-American in the Midwest, Huh has always been inspired by the constantly evolving global conversation about art, design, and culture. She is fascinated by the magic that is created by the merging of many worlds, their varying and sometimes clashing ideas of beauty coming together in new, edited, reinterpreted, and even nuanced ways. This global influence is clear in the rooms Huh creates: British wallpapers mix with Belgian linens; French-cut velvets cover Italian furniture. After combining all of these different furnishings and influences, what emerges is an eclecticism that exemplifies where interior design is headed in the twenty-first century.

THE LOOK: Clean and classic with a dose of modern and pretty elements.

COLOR: To me, color is visual emotion. When a client gives me a sense of how he or she wants to feel in a room, I create a color story around that. Generally, I love colors that feel happy and offer dynamism through contrast. I also like colors that are soothing and calming. There's nothing like being enveloped in a sense of peace.

KEY ELEMENT: Comfortable seating.

ALWAYS HAVE: I am obsessed with fabric, and it is probably my greatest love in decorating. I'm also a china hoarder, and I love a dining table set with white porcelain and beautiful flowers.

INSPIRATION: Instagram! It has completely changed my view on design. Not only can I see all kinds of work from other designers, but I can also see places and details of those places that I may have missed, all from the comfort of my chair.

NEVER FORGET: Start from a foundation of balance, symmetry, and proportion. Then add elements that throw things off a bit to create tension. Try pairing items you may not see together often, such as a Fortuny fabric and a modern chair. No space is complete without something a little bit off—even ugly. It's the tension and conversation between elements that creates compelling beauty.

FROM: Detroit, Michigan

LOCATED IN: New York, New York

INFLUENCES: I'm influenced by many designers, among them Henri Samuel, who created classic formal French interiors, as well as modern and sleek rooms. I also admire Renzo Mongiardino for his command of styles and dedication to artisanship and craftsmen. And I'm influenced by the rooms of Albert Hadley and François Catroux.

A sophisticated harmony is established by mixing the warm neutrals of the wallcovering and ottoman with the cool neutrals of the sofa and rug. The linear patterns throughout heighten the effect.

ABOVE: The red-and-gold Maya Romanoff wallcovering ensures that glamour is the order of the day in this charming master bedroom. To complement the branch motif of the metal bed, a custom cherry blossom print from Tillett Textiles was used for the bed hangings and curtains.

LEFT: Inspired by the world of fine jewelry, Gabriel Scott's dramatic Harlow chandelier holds court in this modern dining room. The handcrafted dining table was purchased at BDDW in Manhattan.

OPPOSITE: This home is on the coast of New Jersey. A relationship between the outdoors and indoors was created by choosing a Cole & Son cloud wallpaper for the ceiling and a hand-painted Fromental branch wallpaper for the walls. A green velvet from Claremont on the sofa completes the theme.

"Robert Couturier once told me that the smallest details can make or break a space. I take that to heart with every project."

AAMIR KHANDWALA

Aamir Khandwala's interest in design dates back to his childhood in Pakistan, when he would spend hours building imaginary houses and structures with his Legos; as a teenager, he would scour the local antiques markets in Karachi to decorate his family home.

Upon moving to New York to attend the Fashion Institute of Technology, Khandwala found himself both overwhelmed and inspired by the city's chaotic frenzy. The culturally diverse worlds of design he experienced continue to inform his work, which was honed while working for his mentor, Robert Couturier.

As a connoisseur of interior furnishings, Khandwala makes spaces come alive with history and provenance, further enhancing them using careful juxtaposition and disciplined layering. The result: rooms with a sense of balance, harmony, and warmth.

KEY ELEMENT: Thoughtfully considered color.

ALWAYS HAVE: A mix of pieces: antique, vintage, and contemporary. Diverse textures—cashmere, wood, chrome—also pique interest.

INSPIRATION: International travel. Recent favorites include the tree-lined avenues of the Condesa neighborhood in Mexico City, which are full of life, and the breathtaking Lake Atitlán in Guatemala, with hand-loomed textiles produced by the women-run weaving co-ops among the Mayan lake communities. Artists also inspire me, including Sol LeWitt, Anish Kapoor, and Terry Winters.

NEVER FORGET: Technology has opened people's eyes to the possibilities and enhancements good design can bring to their lives. But interior design will always be about materials that need to be touched and felt by the human hand.

A whimsical custom mural by Shantell Martin was commissioned to create a unique artwork for this Bellport, New York dining room. The ceramic antler chandelier, faux shagreen—and-bronze dining table, and raffia chairs complete the tableau. A round dyed tatami rug by Nanimarquina works to define the space.

FROM: Karachi, Pakistan

LOCATED IN: New York, New York

INFLUENCES: The voluptuous architectural forms of Oscar Niemeyer, the color sense of India Mahdavi, the warm yet modern approach to furniture of Joaquim Tenreiro, and the inventive eclecticism of David Hicks.

THE LOOK: Timeless, graphic, streamlined yet luxurious.

COLOR: Color is in my DNA, as South Asian culture is full of rich color in clothing, food, home, landscapes . . . it's a part of one's daily life.

OPPOSITE: With its soaring ceiling height, this living room feels welcoming and airy. The semicircular sofa, custom designed for the room, is covered in an Angela Brown Ltd. fabric. Continuing the curved motif are Copa Grande Transitions side tables from Tucker Robbins made from hand-dyed straw. The artwork at right is by Massimo Vitali.

TOP: An artful juxtaposition of shapes and materials animates this stylish kitchen and breakfast room. The concrete tile floor from Ann Sacks and the dining chairs from Moroso keep the space light and breezy.

BOTTOM: The angular lines of the master bedroom and four-poster bed are softened by the arched window and the pattern of the handwoven rug, custom made in Istanbul. The rosewood-and-aluminum nightstand, one of a pair, is American from the 1960s. (left) The clients have a love of Bollywood films, so a custom wallpaper was designed and produced in the style of Andy Warhol for this guest bedroom. The lamp has a concrete base with a perforated-metal shade. (right)

"Being thoroughly prepared is one of the most important attributes for success."

BENNETT LEIFER

Bennett Leifer's aesthetic is guided by his personal mantra: Learn something new every day. That can apply to learning about a new artisan's craft, managing his business, or communicating more successfully. And the rooms he designs reflect those considerations. There is no specific formula, no specific look. He is constantly learning and adapting. That's not to say he doesn't have strong preferences. "I think what makes me a good designer is my ability to evolve and remain flexible," he says.

Leifer studied business and art history at Skidmore College in upstate New York, where he developed an eye for color, composition, and history, as well as an aptitude for balancing a budget and project management. He then spent a decade working for several established design firms, including Juan Pablo Molyneux, whom he credits with teaching him about design history and fine craftsmanship.

When designing this apartment, there was a focus on separating the public spaces from the private ones. In what was once an open layout, custom hand-painted sliding panels were added to separate the family room—just beyond the panels—from the more formal living space. The goal was to give the client flexibility in keeping an open plan for their family, while elegantly separating the spaces when entertaining guests.

FROM: Great Neck, New York

LOCATED IN: New York, New York

INFLUENCES: Karen Knorr's photographs of the palaces and forts of Rajasthan, India. The saturated colors, uniquely characterized by their individual patinas, are breathtaking. Elsa Schiaparelli is influencing a current project I am working on. I am drawn to how she incorporated surrealist art as an accent into something as tactile as fashion. Her work was incredibly intellectual. And Robert Polidori's photography has greatly influenced me, particularly how he captured Versailles.

THE LOOK: Classically influenced rooms that respond to modern life.

COLOR: Color is incredibly subjective. For example, I would describe a woven fabric of two colored threads by their two respective names, whereas other people might see only the overall combination. It's a matter of perception. For me, every tone counts and becomes a cumulative part of the palette. I thoroughly embrace this. Black is an anchoring force and a visual stop sign to draw your eye to its surroundings.

KEY ELEMENT: Something patinaed in every room: age-worn paint on a carved chair, an oxidized bronze table, vintage Fortuny textile cushions. These elements lend an instant sense of history.

ALWAYS HAVE: Jewel tones; lustrous finishes; and sculptural accents.

INSPIRATION: On a recent trip to India, I was struck by the forts and palaces of Rajasthan. The powdery colors and innovative decorative techniques are incredible.

NEVER FORGET: The importance of the phrase "Measure twice, cut once" cannot be overemphasized. I refer to this quote in all aspects of life, but it has a particularly literal translation in the design industry.

OPPOSITE: A custom door was added to separate the sophisticated foyer from the private areas just beyond.

TOP: The concept in this space was to provide intimate dining for a family of four, while allowing for entertaining larger groups. Siting the dining and lounge areas on each side of the mantel created a beautiful view of the fireplace and artwork from the living room.

BOTTOM: This room had flat walls with various recessed architectural niches, to which rhythmic molding details and bookshelves were added for balance. Sconces throughout help to illuminate the space.

*"There's electricity
in great juxtaposition."*

LUCINDA LOYA

Houston, Texas–based designer Lucinda Loya grew up in the small town of Jeffersonville, Indiana. She had a strong work ethic from a young age—by sixteen, she'd had a local newspaper route, been a babysitter, worked as an aerobics instructor, and been a sales associate at a fabric shop. The latter position ignited an interest in pattern and texture. After designing on the side for some friends, including her future husband, Loya opened her own business while simultaneously enrolling in classes at the Art Institute of Houston, where she was intrigued by the study of antiquities and their history.

Comfortable designing in varied styles—contemporary, transitional, classic—and combinations, Loya creates rooms that might include Colonial-style painted floors, midcentury chrome chairs, and patterned wallpaper. It's a modern mix that is both refreshing and intriguing.

FROM: Jeffersonville, Indiana

LOCATED IN: Houston, Texas

INFLUENCES: My work is influenced by anyone who thinks outside of the box and is willing to take chances. The iconic fashion designer Martin Margiela's classic-with-a-twist approach is a big inspiration. I would put Libertine, Vivienne Westwood, and Alexander McQueen in the same category.

THE LOOK: Timeless, sophisticated, and livable.

COLOR: I most often rely on my clients' preferences with regard to color. But if a request does not come from the client, we offer inspirational images, rugs, and, of course, works of art to get a sense of what

A blue canvas by New York–based artist Craig Alan establishes this formal living room's color scheme which is carried through on the sofa bolsters and the vase on the custom side table. The coffee table was made using a smoked-glass mirror.

they respond to. Speaking for myself, I'm often inspired by the runway, as I'm very attuned to fashion.

KEY ELEMENTS: Every successful room requires character, which is the sum total of all its furnishings. But of equal importance is maintaining balance, proportion, and scale for a visually pleasing atmosphere.

ALWAYS HAVE: I believe in integrating something white into every space. It provides the eye with a point of reference for the other colors in the room. And I include something in a room that telegraphs a sense of humor or anything that takes a client to a happy place.

INSPIRATION: I am a lover of art and fashion! I stay current by attending industry fairs like High Point in North Carolina, Salone del Mobile in Milan, and Maison&Objet and Déco Off in Paris, among others. I frequent the art fairs like Miami's Art Basel and the Armory Shows in New York, to name a few.

NEVER FORGET: Mix things up, but remember: if something is old, then appreciate it; if it is new, it should have clean lines. And I am not a fan of replicas. Originality speaks volumes in design.

TOP: Soaring windows flood this den with glorious light. The Murano-glass chandelier adds a touch of femininity to the room, while the boxy custom club chairs, upholstered in blue velvet, add just the right amount of color.

BOTTOM: The graphic overscale wallpaper in this powder room, featuring pixelated flowers, adds personality to a small space. (left) Contrasting materials create visual interest and a bit of drama in this stylish dining room. (right)

OPPOSITE: A joyful riot of shapes and colors greets visitors in the entry of this Houston home. The linear-patterned wallpaper accentuates the hardware of the custom credenza.

"A well-designed home is meant to comfort, function, and dazzle all at the same time."

PATRICK MELE

During his years at New York University, Patrick Mele worked first for Kate and Andy Spade and then for Ralph Lauren. From these powerhouses and the creative people who worked with them, he learned how to tell a story through design. "The way they created a collection and built an ad campaign is very much the way I conceive of an interior," Mele says. "My design work is always plot- and personality-driven. I want my rooms to tell a particular story." During these formative years, Mele also had the good fortune to work with creative force Richard Lambertson. They collaborated on the second incarnation of a design-and-lifestyle shop that Lambertson founded called Privet House.

Mele says that the people he worked with during his early career all had one thing in common: style. The ways they walked, talked, and dressed, and their tastes in music, art, and furniture, were fully formed. Each possessed a strong point of view and knew how to live. These are the qualities Mele carries with him and hopes to impart to his clients.

The family room in this Westchester County, New York, home was designed around antique Persian carpets that the clients brought back from their honeymoon in Istanbul. The kilim on the ottoman features colors from the rug, while the sofa and club chair provide visually interesting contrast. Black is also in the mix on the wing chair, the fireplace surround, and the striped wallpaper in the adjacent dining room.

FROM: Greenwich, Connecticut

LOCATED IN: New York, New York

INFLUENCES: First and foremost, growing up in a creative, design-obsessed, entrepreneurial family. When I think of a great American designer, Albert Hadley is the pinnacle. His approach was timeless and classic, yet always gutsy. There was nothing prim about an Albert Hadley room. Madeleine Castaing defined Parisian chic; her vision was strong, feminine, and glamorous. Charles Sevigny is such an elegant, worldly man. I admire the astute knowledge of fine and decorative arts he wove into each of his projects.

And I love David Hicks for his showmanship and his masterful way with color, lighting, and a good dose of drama. Angelo Donghia created the kind of modern, sexy, strong rooms that I love to be in—rooms for grown-ups, nighttime rooms.

THE LOOK: Exuberant and comfortable, with a dash of humor.

COLOR: I favor rich, saturated color. A variety of tints and shades of the same color will make a room bounce. I also like punctuation marks of ebony and ivory sprinkled throughout any space. Art and fashion inspire my color sense. I love the Fauvist movement for its color and expression, strong brushstrokes, and painterly quality.

KEY ELEMENT: Lighting that does not follow trends. Beautiful lighting is perhaps the most essential quality in any room. Every light should be on a dimmer, and every bulb warm in tone. My favorite lampshades are made from either antique Indian saris or stark opaque paper. The former provides a romantic effect; the latter is more architectural.

ALWAYS HAVE: Comfortable, well-made upholstery with a mixture of skirts and legs: I loathe a room constricted by only one or the other.

INSPIRATION: Sitting at a café or restaurant and watching the show go on! A bustling restaurant is like no other place in the world: filled with

gorgeous people having some of the best moments of their days and enjoying life.

NEVER FORGET: Not everyone who calls upon a decorator or interior designer possesses a fully formed aesthetic or sensibility. It is our job to help them mold and create their own through the expression of their home.

OPPOSITE: This charming vestibule carries the theme of the adjacent garden room into the house. A trompe l'oeil painted table is populated with marble urn lamps stenciled with the clients' initial. The English needlepoint bench and African mask are from Mele's shop in Greenwich, Connecticut.

TOP: Black, white, cream, gold, and shades of green welcome visitors into the glamorous entrance of this classic 1920s shingled home. An Empire table sits proudly in the middle of room, and a 1920s French crystal-and-bronze chandelier hangs above it. A mahogany baby grand piano off-center creates an opportunity for the space to double as a music room.

CENTER: This grown-up but comfortable living room is lovely during the day, but designed for optimal impact in the evening. Its moody pea-green custom wall color sets the theme for the space. A 1970s overscale Ming-style coffee table atop a zebra-skin rug anchors the room.

BOTTOM: A nineteenth-century patinaed copper street lantern from Philadelphia hangs over the black-lacquered island in this classic working kitchen. Subway tiles, stainless steel appliances, and a framed century-old American flag complete the space.

> *"A home should be a place to rest, to get away, to entertain, and to be with family. All of the items in a room should hum together to create that peace."*

WESLEY MOON

New York City–based designer Wesley Moon is self-admittedly obsessed with all things design. "Design is at the core of everything I love and do," he says. "When I vacation, I always go to see at least one historic home. When I read, it's usually a design magazine or book, or historical fiction with something beautiful about its setting or characters. Beauty, and being surrounded by it, is everything to me." That passion shows in his work.

Moon studied architecture at Georgia Tech and then transferred to the American InterContinental University to get his degree in interior design. In 2000, he was offered a position at Skidmore, Owings & Merrill. Moon subsequently moved to New York City, where he met his first client through a friend; he struck out on his own in 2008 with Wesley Moon, Inc.

The John Saladino banquette in the corner of the great room is a cozy spot to curl up with a good book. The vintage Mazzega glass floor lamp by Carlo Nason was found on 1stdibs; the chair, one of a pair, is a nineteenth-century Louis XVI with the original Aubusson panel on the back. The custom fur rug visually defines the seating area.

FROM: Buford, Georgia

LOCATED IN: New York, New York

INFLUENCES: I think my design aesthetic is really a reaction to the cumulative experiences I have encountered my whole life. Every time I open a shelter magazine or visit the Paris flea market or see a piece of well-designed furniture, I catalog what I find to be visually exciting. Eventually, that inspiration, distilled with influences from my very colorful childhood, will show up in my work in some way or another.

THE LOOK: Personalized, detailed, collected, and ethereal.

COLOR: I am attracted to deep, saturated colors, but many clients are afraid of color. When I get one who isn't, I really go wild. If a client wants a more neutral palette, I work in soft complementary tones to ensure a room is never flat.

KEY ELEMENT: Balance. The visual volume of a room should be at the same level, and everything must be in equilibrium. Color, proportion, visual weight: they all have to work together to create a harmonious environment.

ALWAYS HAVE: Throw pillows do wonders to bring in just a bit of whatever you need to finish off that balance I mentioned above. Carefully curated accessories warm up the space and make it feel full. I'm not big into tchotchkes and bookcases are for books, but I add selected pieces that represent the client in some way: something they love, something from somewhere they've traveled.

INSPIRATION: Most recently my partner, Sal, and I were in Puerto Vallarta, Mexico, for New Year's, and we were impressed by the crafts made and sold by the local residents. We purchased two blankets that we brought back, had sewn together, and now use as our living room rug. We also purchased a hanging ceramic sculpture that's so chic; we love it and will be hanging it in our Fire Island home this summer.

NEVER FORGET: Mixing styles of furniture and textiles, if done in a balanced way, gives the feeling that the room has evolved over time, which is comforting and personal.

OPPOSITE: An ethereal mural by Dean Barger softened the original paneling of the room. The French 1940s Louis XVI–style ebonized commode and the Victorian bamboo chair are both from Newel; the artwork is by Robert Rauschenberg. Blush silk curtains add a feminine touch.

TOP: To complement the existing rock wall, a Jean de Merry sofa with a walnut frame and brass legs covered in a blush suede was added; the pillows are linen velvet. A vintage Paul Frankl cork-top coffee table, custom shearling-covered slipper chairs, and sisal carpet complete the neutral envelope.

BOTTOM: The vision for this room was a contemporary Alpine chalet. MJ Atelier was commissioned to create large murals on canvas with raised plaster detailing at either end of the room depicting mountains with animals and foliage indigenous to the Alps. Three intimate sitting areas plus the bar create a human scale. Accessories include a set of ceramic tulips by Matthew Solomon from Maison Gerard; the bronze lamps on the consoles are from Valerie Goodman Gallery.

"Rooms should be like people: expressive, individual, no two the same."

EMILIE MUNROE

For her tenth birthday, Emilie Munroe's parents allowed her to choose new bedding, and her career as a designer was born. The new sheets, shams, and duvet completely transformed the look and feel of her room. That same feeling of pride and excitement remains to this day when she walks into a space she has created. Munroe is very clear that she has no particular design style. But there are constants: her rooms are youthful, accessible, colorful, and comfortable.

She was introduced to this perspective while rising through the ranks at Jay Jeffers's San Francisco design firm. The signature color and whimsy of Jeffers's work was design eye candy; even if the color schemes were neutral, he maintained an undercurrent of warmth and joy. Munroe endeavors to do the same.

strength and whimsy throughout. The foundation of this signature feeling is a balance of both masculine and feminine elements. Color (or lack thereof), texture, and materials are curated so that a home is neither too precious nor too serious, but instead reaches a delicate equilibrium. Sometimes this balance is found within one room, but often we review the home as a whole and create individual spaces that embody complementary tones.

KEY ELEMENT: No matter the scope of the job, we find a way to include a statement pendant light or chandelier. Decorative lighting is the jewelry of the house and makes a huge impact in any room, but especially in the entry, dining room, and bedrooms.

ALWAYS HAVE: Unexpected, conversation-starting patterns are my specialty, but I also install many interesting natural-fiber textures in rooms to bring a subtle softness and interest to the spaces. I look at mirrors as interior-facing windows because they reflect both scenery and light. You have to be careful not to over-mirror a space, but every room can have one, as long as it's properly scaled and mixed in nicely with art.

INSPIRATION: Much of my inspiration is currently gleaned in the comfort of my own home—dare I say my own bedroom—immersed in the magical worlds of film and premium cable shows. From Wes Anderson's incredible

This entry was added to the house during construction. The walnut wrapped around the window-seat bench highlights the cozy nook and coordinates with other touches of natural walnut throughout the house. The large window was frosted for privacy, but includes a band of transparent glass around the edge for clarity and light. Both the window seat and floor-to-ceiling built-ins provide much-needed coat and shoe storage for the family and their guests.

FROM: Los Altos, California

LOCATED IN: San Francisco, California

INFLUENCES: Fashion's ability to influence culture—to reinvent and reimagine—has always captivated me, especially when it comes to mixing a few unexpected colors, textures, or shapes into a classic look to make it totally unique. Gwen Stefani's L.A.M.B. and J.Crew under Jenna Lyons are two favorite brands.

THE LOOK: Eclectic, detailed, and unexpectedly luxurious.

COLOR: Color, always color! I love bringing color into a space, but even if the scheme is ivory and gray, I will design a room to feel refreshing and unique with elements of both

retro-inspired sets to *Westworld*'s wild sci-fi futurism, inspiring visual imagery is right at our fingertips.

NEVER FORGET: For all the current focus on technology, I think the next phase of luxury is disconnection. Perhaps that means a room or even a wing of the house where mobile devices and computers don't work, or vacation homes that are 100 percent off the grid.

OPPOSITE: A metal fireplace surround is the modern textural contrast to a reclaimed-beam mantel and built-in bookshelves. This material mix adds an edge to the bohemian feel of the space. Existing chairs were reimagined in new cobalt linen upholstery with contrasting jute trim. Mixed black and brass metals keep the room relaxed and approachable, with the color blue anchoring the space.

TOP: The sculptural table base is organized and curvaceous, while the large-scale papier-mâché chandelier above is more organic and free-form. The dining space is defined by a round woven area rug. The mix of chair colors adds whimsy and connects the room stylistically to the adjacent entryway.

CENTER: This colorful woven hanging chair is cozied up with a mix of patterned and fluffy throw pillows. The painted wainscot treatment adds architectural interest to the space. (left) In this guest bath, the design started with the graphic black-and-white patterned floor tile. Neutral backgrounds allow reinvention by adjusting the hues of accessories. (right)

BOTTOM: A curated mix of color, pattern, and texture provides a warm, collected feel in this master bedroom. A walnut bed frame, metal nightstands, plaster lamps, and a natural-fiber rug all act as neutrals when mixed with more saturated hues.

"I don't believe in safe decorating."

NICK OLSEN

As a young boy growing up in northwest Florida, Nick Olsen was an insatiable creative with an eye for perfection. In between swim team practice and tennis lessons, he would build neo-Georgian dollhouses for his older sister. As a teen, it was his fascination with fashion, shelter, and travel magazines that brought his future career in decorating into focus. Most of all, he was obsessed with houses. In his small neighborhood in Pensacola, Florida, there were wonderful examples of late Victorian, Arts and Crafts, Mediterranean, Tudor, and Renaissance Revival homes filling the oak tree–lined blocks. Olsen studied their nuances in Virginia and Lee McAlester's *A Field Guide to American Houses*.

While at Columbia University studying architecture, Olsen came across decorator Miles Redd's NoHo townhouse in *W* magazine and wrote the storied designer a fan letter, leading to a five-year stint working with him. In 2010, Olsen established his own firm.

FROM: Pensacola, Florida

LOCATED IN: New York, New York

INFLUENCES: I began my career working for Miles Redd, who once worked for Bunny Williams, who once worked for Albert Hadley and Sister Parish. I'm humbled to be part of that lineage. They all influence me. When I look at a Parish-Hadley, Bunny, or Miles room, I see an inviting mix of classicism, comfort, creativity, and connoisseurship—the four Cs.

THE LOOK: Stylish, comfortable, and charismatic.

COLOR: I love using color and find inspiration in nature. The combinations are limitless. But an entirely grisaille-painted or parchment-clad room can

Olsen chose a multicolored Moroccan rug to set the color scheme in this family room. Ethnic patterns and animal prints are interspersed with enough breathing room in the form of neutral walls, sofas, and a large indoor-outdoor carpet. The room's massive Florian Baudrexel sculpture, purchased years before at an art fair, *just* fits above the fireplace. The oak-and-rush side chairs are in the style of Charlotte Perriand, and the leopard linen on the slipper chairs is by Rose Cumming.

be just as chic if not more chic than a kaleidoscopic one. I don't believe in safe decorating, so I'm always working with new and unusual color combinations.

KEY ELEMENT: The floor plan! I always start with a detailed furniture plan. I listen to my clients and observe how they live and want to live. Rooms need to be organized around activities, and the floor plan makes sense of them all.

ALWAYS HAVE: The biggest common thread of my work is scale. I will find a mirror so big that it grazes the ceiling, or hang the most delicate painting above a gutsy Georgian fireplace mantel. Bold gestures that do not overwhelm—that's my ethos.

INSPIRATION: Travel. As a ten-year-old, I had a subscription to *Islands* magazine. As an adult, I've gotten lost in the Marrakech souks and swum through secret cenotes in Mexico. The mental images I collect inform my work.

NEVER FORGET: Contrast. I'm drawn to it: I love lacquer next to plaster, straw next to mirror, floral next to geometric, and so on. Sir John Richardson, the famed Picasso biographer, said he needed something ugly in every room, or else it all looked like too much "ghastly good taste." I agree.

OPPOSITE: In this space between the formal dining room and living room, the bold pattern of the herringbone floor plays off a simple grass-cloth wallpaper with flecks of red and blue.

TOP: The client's own sconces were given a verdigris finish by artist Agustin Hurtado, and a pair of midcentury lounge chairs were re-covered in David Kaihoi's Turkish Step fabric for Schumacher.

BOTTOM: In the pool house, Benjamin Moore's Chrome Green on the lower cabinets is echoed in the Moroccan rugs in this space. (left) The restful palette of this teen girl's room gets its color from the Imogen Heath linen on the headboard and roman shades.(right)

BRIAN PAQUETTE

With an education in painting and conceptual art, Seattle-based interior designer Brian Paquette has an aesthetic unique among his peers. He possesses an innate understanding of color that's informed by both his studies and by the Pacific Northwest locale in which he works. His rooms feel like they exemplify the adage of bringing the outdoors in, with colors and textures pulled from nature.

After completing an MFA in painting and art history, Paquette began as the glorified delivery driver for a decorator in his hometown of Newport, Rhode Island. The homes he worked in were nods to Billy Baldwin and Elsie de Wolfe, with pattern on pattern and sisal rugs. It was through this job that Paquette fell in love with design, learning about the lifestyle and the history of these families and their homes and the idea of "appropriate" decorating. As much as he loved the work, he grew tired of small-town life. He made his way to the West Coast, working as a sample librarian for a textile and furniture showroom and in contemporary furniture, and eventually started his own firm with the support of countless designers. Paquette believes in the value of close, collaborative relationships with both his clients and the coterie of local craftsmen he relies on to realize his design vision.

On the contemporary side are Joseph Dirand, Pamela Shamshiri, Jean-Louis Deniot, Peter Dunham, Commune Design, Jamie Bush, and Olson Kundig.

THE LOOK: Traditional floor plans inflected with a mix of contemporary furnishings.

COLOR: I like to build palettes based on the natural elements outside the home. I tend toward colors that feel as if the pigment has been kissed by dirt or the earth.

KEY ELEMENTS: Sculptural lighting, layered rugs, and art—always art.

ALWAYS HAVE: Natural elements: wood, stone, cowhide, wool. Making a strong connection between nature and the built environment is paramount to successful rooms.

INSPIRATION: The quiet winter mornings in Seattle, sitting with a cup of coffee before the race of the day; the vast beauty of a sunset on the Oregon coast; the confidence of artists from all over the world to expose themselves on canvas.

NEVER FORGET: Don't neglect the everyday details of a home. From where you drop the mail and keys to where the soap and kitchen utensils sit to the coasters, bookends, and guest towels—all of these details should live up to the home surrounding them. They must be both functional and beautiful.

An austere dining table is paired with custom upholstered chairs from Paquette's collection for Lawson-Fenning. The curtains and Roman shade, in a sheer textile from Nobilis, filter the abundant sunlight.

FROM: Newport, Rhode Island

LOCATED IN: Seattle, Washington

INFLUENCES: The juxtaposition of traditional design with the work of more modern or contemporary designers is what has informed my work the most. On the traditional side are Markham Roberts, Billy Baldwin, Steven Gambrel, and Ashley Whittaker.

OPPOSITE: A subtle mix of warm neutral colors and textures harmonizes in this living room. The sofa was custom designed by Paquette, while the vintage Japanese Tansu cabinet adds a sense of history.

TOP: A Lawson-Fenning bed upholstered in a Glant fabric harmonizes perfectly with graphic bedding by Hollywood at Home. The dresser is from Room & Board, and the artworks to the left of the doorway are by Sol LeWitt.

BOTTOM: The ceramics on this kitchen counter are from a collaboration by Natasha Alphonse and Paquette, and the framed artwork is a vintage find. (left) A figure painting by Anthony Cudahy, a lamp from Stone and Sawyer, and a vintage vase create a stylish tableau. (right)

TINA RAMCHANDANI

After graduating with a degree in interior design from the Art Institute of Philadelphia, Tina Ramchandani began her professional career working for Frank & Marcotullio, a New York–based commercial design firm, where she learned how to manage projects and stay organized. After three years, Ramchandani decided to shift gears and focus on residential design. She considers herself lucky to have landed a position with legendary New York designer Vicente Wolf. "During my five years at Vicente Wolf's firm, I was influenced by his sense of style, his serene aesthetic, and his problem-solving methods," she says. "I also learned to trust my instincts, have confidence in myself and my work, and own my decisions. He truly allowed me to hone my sense of style. Without this, I would not have been able to launch my firm."

That confidence comes through in Ramchandani's rooms, as does the clean-lined serenity she learned from Wolf. The simplest design solutions require exceptionally careful thought: with fewer objects in a space, the selection and placement of each item becomes of paramount importance. Ramchandani consistently proves herself a master of the task.

Cognac leather chairs inspired the dining area's color palette in this West Village pied-à-terre. The artwork and accessories continue the theme, while the Lee Broom pendant adds a bit of glamour to the space.

FROM: Edison, New Jersey

LOCATED IN: New York, New York

INFLUENCES: In terms of historical designers, I reference David Hicks, Billy Baldwin, and Elsie de Wolfe in my work. Some of the contemporary talents I look to include Piet Boon, Philippe Starck, Joseph Dirand, Tristan Auer, Jean-Louis Deniot, John Saladino, and fashion designer Tom Ford, for his remarkable style.

THE LOOK: Soulful minimalism—warm and modern.

COLOR: When using color, I think it's important to commit, make a statement, and have a driving vision. I try to infuse various shades of the color in several ways: layered; on the walls, ceiling, floors, and furniture; and in accents and accessories.

KEY ELEMENT: Proper lighting, hands down, as it immediately dictates how a room makes you feel upon entering. Each room will have different lighting requirements, but a successful room is lit well, not too dimly, and not too brightly; it also has accents of light throughout the room.

ALWAYS HAVE: Black: either pops of it as an accent, or as a grand neutral color throughout the design

INSPIRATION: I travel quite a bit, and I try to visit a museum, a garden, or the home of an artist when I go to a new city. When I traveled to Barcelona for the first time, Park Güell, designed by renowned architect Antoni Gaudí, was my only requirement, and although I anticipated it would be beautiful, it truly blew me away. Gaudí thought about every aspect of the experience,

from the intricate details to the way you can get lost in the park to the views. The visit made me realize that design is an experience and about so much more than simply an aesthetically pleasing space, which I'm always mindful of during my design process.

NEVER FORGET: Scale is one of the most misunderstood elements of design. Not only does a piece of furniture have to fill a room properly, it also needs to be layered to add interest. I achieve this through varying furniture heights, large area rugs that take up the majority of the room, and floor mirrors that are the correct height and do not feel as though they are sitting low on the wall. The wrong scale creates an undertone of chaos and makes those in the room feel uneasy, while proper scale, size, and height allow those in the room to feel relaxed.

TOP: A custom raw-steel coffee table with a blackened finish and bronze seams anchors the living room, which is awash in neutral finishes. The television takes on a sculptural feeling when hung directly across from the painting on the right.

BOTTOM: To continue the tailored look, accents of black were added via the leather of the barstools. The streamlined cabinetry and island work together to create a serene backdrop for cooking and entertaining.

OPPOSITE: A muted, neutral putty color on all surfaces of the master bedroom works to maintain the flow. A Phillip Jeffries grass-cloth wallcovering introduces an organic element.

ELIZABETH PYNE SINGER

"Respect the past, enjoy the present, look forward to the future" is the motto at McMillen Inc., the oldest decorating firm in America. And Elizabeth Pyne Singer, daughter of the firm's current president, Ann Pyne, is part of that future.

Having worked as a specialist in the old master paintings department at Sotheby's, Singer brought an emphasis on the importance of connoisseurship with her when she joined McMillen in 2009. Her experience at Sotheby's taught her to look at every antique, piece of furniture, light fixture, and fabric in person before recommending it to a client.

With a staff of ten designers, McMillen has a range of aesthetic sensibilities and a common emphasis on classicism, restraint, and personality. Where does Singer fit in? "I would say that my personal style is playful," she says. "I love color, patterns, texture, furniture with whimsical details, and beautiful objects."

In this dining room, a three-dimensional Sydney Butchkes work contrasts with a painting by Robert Duran. Schumacher wallpaper and furniture purchased at auction, in concert with the artworks, spark conversation.

FROM: New York, New York

LOCATED IN: New York, New York

INFLUENCES: My favorite historical designer is Samuel Marx, and I could spend hours looking at Liz O'Brien's book *Ultramodern Samuel Marx: Architect, Designer, Art Collector.* The most powerful influence on my work is my mother. She has taught me everything about the discipline of interior design, and she trained my eye. I've accompanied her and my late grandmother, Betty Sherrill, to antiques shows, furniture dealers, and other people's houses for as long as I can remember. (And if you know my mother, you know she has something to say about everything we see!)

THE LOOK: Carefully thought-out, deliberate, tailored, and timeless.

COLOR: Since there is almost no color I don't like, when we start a project, we often turn to our clients for the initial color schemes. I think what people sometimes don't realize is that there has to be a flow of color between rooms—that one room should relate to the next. A room that is teal will look wonderful next to a gray, yellow, or purple room, but it will not work next to a room decorated in a rusty orange.

KEY ELEMENTS: Woven wood shades, textured walls, and a fireplace surround whose height is in proportion to the ceiling height and furniture in the room. And every room I design has at least one gilt object. But the gilding must be subtle—beware of cheap-looking "radiator-paint" gold!

ALWAYS HAVE: Good proportions. In a room that lacks proportion, decorating becomes a way to solve a problem—you have to manipulate the decorating in order to cover up the inherent flaws of the space. On the other hand, in a room with good proportions, where the space already feels right, the decorating can be much more flexible.

INSPIRATION: I keep my eyes open and take photographs everywhere that I am, even in less-than-obvious places. For example, recently, at the Musée Nissim de Camondo in Paris I did not find the most relevant inspiration in the elaborate and beautiful bas-relief carving of the drawing room's paneling, but in the geometric painted doors of the museum's audiovisual room.

NEVER FORGET: It is possible to tell the quality of an object from a photo, but only if you've seen other versions of the object in the flesh over and over again.

ABOVE: A painting by Bernard Pfriem is flanked by a pair of abstract canvases by John Ferren in this sophisticated New York living room. The colors of the rug, chairs, and sofa—upholstered in Clarence House's Tibet linen pattern—complement the artworks.

OPPOSITE: Two works by American abstract painter Leon Polk Smith hang above the bed in this lively bedroom. The Oriental sensibility is accentuated by a hand-blocked wallpaper from Farrow & Ball, and the Roman shade fabric is from Schumacher.

"A beautiful interior is not just something we see, it is something we experience. A well-designed space engages the senses and nourishes the soul."

JOSHUA SMITH

Unique among his young-designer peers, Joshua Smith takes a holistic approach to design. A graduate of the New York School of Interior Design and an alumnus of Steven Gambrel's firm, Smith considers not just form and decoration, but also how spirituality affects his clients, placing him in a design continuum with Clodagh, who has built a career around that idea.

Rooms that telegraph comfort—ones meant for easy, everyday life—are the hallmark of Smith's work. Subtle color palettes, thoughtfully considered floor plans, furniture with gorgeous patina, and including his clients in the design process are crucial. He says, "At the beginning of each project, I take my clients through an in-depth process that clearly defines their style and conception of beauty. All decisions moving forward tie back to this process, so that the interior becomes a beautiful kaleidoscope of materials and furnishings that are representative of who they are and how they live."

THE LOOK: Classic, comfortable, edited.

COLOR: There's more to color than pigment. Color evokes feelings and creates mood, and there's a sacredness to all colors. Blues and greens are calming and grounding. Reds are energizing. Grays bring balance. Yellows, cheerfulness and creativity. Pinks, romance and love. So when thinking of color schemes for rooms, I ask the client, "How do you want to *feel* in this room?" I rarely use bold colors on walls—I save those for accents. With the stressors of everyday modern life, we are all overstimulated. Studies have shown that soothing colors calm the central nervous system.

KEY ELEMENT: A spiritual connection to our homes. I believe that when we seek to improve the relationship between the body, mind, and soul, there is a tendency to overlook the role our environments play in enhancing the quality of our lives. It's a fact that our homes affect all aspects of our lives.

ALWAYS HAVE: A cashmere throw— it provides instant coziness and a way to dress up furniture! Candles make everything more beautiful, create a sense of sacredness, and can freshen the room with subtle fragrance. And a touch of blue references the sky or the ocean for a subtle connection to nature.

FROM: Crosby, Texas

LOCATED IN: New York, New York and Litchfield County, Connecticut

INFLUENCES: I love the soft color, lightness, and airiness of a neoclassical Robert Adam interior. Along those same lines, Elsie de Wolfe's philosophy resonates. Her departure from the fussiness of the Victorian period inspired a more streamlined style. And furniture-wise, nothing lights me up like an eighteenth- or nineteenth-century French or Belgian table or case good, smooth as talc and with a patina that has stories to tell.

This generous screened porch measures eighteen feet by twenty-eight feet, with a twelve-foot-high ceiling, to accommodate large gatherings of friends and family, while maximizing the connection between the landscape and the indoors. The stones that make up the fireplace were collected from the homeowner's property.

INSPIRATION: Inspiration often originates from travels, artwork, and textiles, but I have learned over the years that it truly is all around us. Mother Nature continues to be the ultimate inspiration for me—no one does color combinations better!

NEVER FORGET: Including art in an interior is of paramount importance, and Agnes Martin is my favorite artist. I also love Richard Diebenkorn, Paul Klee, and Pablo Picasso. Visit museums, such as the Musée Rodin in Paris, and the Menil Collection in Houston, as well as outdoor spaces like the grounds of the Grand Trianon and Petit Trianon at Versailles.

TOP: Abundant sunlight streams through this living room at all hours of the day. The furnishings were carefully edited to allow the negative spaces to maintain the airy sensibility of the house.

CENTER: The entry stair hall was designed to be a glimpse of the overall experience of the home: subtle yet complex color schemes set a breezy tone. (left) Nothing beats a crisp, white bathroom for feeling calm, serene, and clean. And no farmhouse is complete without a soaking tub to relieve the stressors of the day. This one is in perfect harmony with its surroundings, painted in Benjamin Moore White Dove. (right)

BOTTOM: Antique French blue-striped linens make for the perfect bed pillows in this quiet master bedroom. The key to mixing stripes is to vary the size and alternate the background colors.

OPPOSITE: This dining room features a French trestle-style farm table from the nineteenth century paired with midcentury chairs that share its simple aesthetic. Six different paint colors in the space speak of a subtle sophistication that is revealed over time.

MICHELLE R. SMITH

Renovating and decorating have been Michelle R. Smith's hobbies since she was a child. She remembers when she was six, the local paint store started selling decorative wallpaper borders. She had a chair rail installed in her bedroom immediately, and she and her mom changed the border once a year. The Christmas gift she requested at age eleven? Changing the tile in her bathroom.

Yet Smith took a circuitous path to her design career, beginning with law school and a subsequent job with a big firm. A partner there asked her to help him with his apartment, and then a chance meeting with Daniel Romualdez led her to an internship at the decorator's firm. That internship turned into a job, and the rest is history.

As for personal aesthetics? Smith sees her work as ever evolving with her clients. Change may be a constant, but all of her projects have two things in common: visual appeal and high style.

FROM: Morgan City, Louisiana

LOCATED IN: New York, New York

INFLUENCES: My mother, who renovated and decorated our homes as a hobby. Her enthusiasm for decorating is something I always admired.

THE LOOK: Sophisticated, yet comfortable and inviting.

COLOR: I tend toward washed-out colors rather than bold ones. I am a sucker for a light blue that skews gray or a light green that might be kind of tan. Some people see a beige or neutral room, but I see the undertone. For example, in my house now, I will tell someone that something is in the blue room or the pink room, and there's a fifty-fifty chance they'll know that the rooms are different colors.

KEY ELEMENT: Sconces! When planning a new project or a renovation, it's very rare that I'll design a room without wall sconces. They draw the eye down from the ceiling to the level where all the action happens: art, furniture, door hardware, light switches.

ALWAYS HAVE: I love vintage bowls to collect clutter, a pair of urns if we have the right surface for them, art framed in unexpected ways, and matching lampshades throughout the room.

INSPIRATION: Inspiration can be so overwhelming these days! I guess I'm inspired by the rooms I've been in that were comfortable and felt the most collected over time. For my clients, I like to have them bring me their inspirations from their own lives, and then I like to interpret those inspirations in my own language. If I am successful, the finished product becomes something unique to the client.

NEVER FORGET: As the twenty-first century unfolds, aesthetically good design is easier and easier to attain. Lately, with the inundation of inspiration images from Pinterest and Instagram, I think it's important to find inspiration in singular things, like an antique piece of furniture or a vintage textile, or maybe a bowl. If it's beautiful, you can build an entire room around it.

The wide-plank pine floors and mantelpiece were original to this Sag Harbor, New York, cottage, so antique furnishings were chosen to complement the home's inherent history. A contemporary chandelier provides a counterpoint, and the *tulipiere* is vintage.

OPPOSITE: Perfect for summer entertaining, this screened porch is outfitted with vintage light fixtures, a simple farmhouse table, and weathered wicker chairs. The pale-green floor echoes the surrounding moss just outside.

TOP: Grass-green club chairs populate the living room seating area, with its view into the adjacent guest room. Vintage textiles are perfectly in keeping with the age of the house. The contemporary chrome lamp adds a modern touch.

BOTTOM: The open kitchen shelves provide an opportunity to display tableware collections, and the scalloped wood valance adds a decorative flourish. Custom cabinetry below echoes the farmhouse feel. (left) On the other side of the kitchen, a commercial stove was chosen for clients who love to cook. Curved shelves soften the room's corners. (right)

CRAIG STRULOVITZ

Growing up with an interest in all things creative, Craig Strulovitz started watercolor-painting classes at age five. Throughout his childhood, he spent as much time as possible studying the arts: drawing, painting, photography, ceramics, and all things visual.

Strulovitz always had a fascination with rooms; one of his favorite places to visit as a child was his grandfather's home office. He was a custom-home builder, and Strulovitz would spend hours flipping through floor plans, trying to visualize the spaces and designing the "perfect" house in his head.

After earning an undergraduate degree in interior architecture from the Rhode Island School of Design, Strulovitz settled in New York City, where he found a position at Glenn Gissler Design. He honed his skills under Gissler's mentorship; thirteen years later he holds the position of senior designer at the firm.

FROM: West Milford, New Jersey

LOCATED IN: New York, New York

INFLUENCES: The pioneering early-twentieth-century modern designers and architects, such as Josef Hoffmann, Adolf Loos, and Carlo Scarpa. These innovators moved away from decoration and ornamentation to focus more on proportion, superb natural materials, patterns, and textures.

THE LOOK: Modern interiors inspired by historical design movements.

COLOR: I prefer colors from nature— the bright green of new-growth leaves in the spring or the deep blues of the ocean on a clear day.

KEY ELEMENT: A well-designed room starts with having a great furniture plan. When beginning the design process, think about the function of each space and develop a layout incorporating all of those functions.

ALWAYS HAVE: A well-considered seating arrangement that feels inviting for one person, but can easily accommodate large groups. Get the best-quality, most comfortable sofa your budget will allow. Then incorporate smaller chairs and ottomans that can be easily moved around for a variety of different-size groups.

INSPIRATION: I often find inspiration in the composition of extraordinary artwork. In interior design, like any visual art, you need to pay attention to shape and proportion, balance, and harmony among the elements. There must be exciting elements that pull your focus but also negative space for your eyes to rest on.

NEVER FORGET: Storage. If you have thirty pairs of shoes or five hundred books, you should know where they are going to go. When everything has its place, your design will feel resolved and successful.

Upon entering this apartment, you first see a bold composition featuring Theodoros Stamos's 1946 painting *The Sacrifice* above a circa-1830 Chinese altar table. The pair of upholstered stools are covered in a soft green fabric to complement the palette in the adjacent rooms. The composition is completed by a curated arrangement of objects, including a rustic African sculpture and a Tiffany Studios candlestick.

OPPOSITE: The open-plan dining area has a large mirror to further expand the feeling of space. Above the dining table hangs an organic Lindsey Adelman Branching Bubble chandelier to contrast with the square-edged furniture in dark-stained walnut.

ABOVE: The large and vibrant painting by Larry Poons above the custom sofa adds an element of surprise to the room's neutral palette. The sofa is flanked by a pair of 1950s Italian lamps with an ombré glaze.

RIGHT: To create a distinction between spaces, the family room was painted a soft green, complementing the background color of prints by Jo Baer on the walls. A white Nelson Saucer pendant adds a rich luminosity to the space.

"Every room should have contrast and a bit of tension."

LAURA UMANSKY

Laura Umansky's interiors are always client-centric and site-specific. She believes that telling the homeowners' personal story is paramount and understanding their surroundings is the bedrock of a successful room. Umansky learned a lot from her father, who designed and built two of her childhood homes himself, even though he wasn't a trained architect. "I watched the process happen from start to finish and was inspired by the possibility of doing the same," she says. "From a young age, I was heavily influenced by my environment, always organizing and arranging my possessions with intention and purpose."

Now, with an educational background in architecture, Umansky enjoys learning more about how things are connected and put together: the tectonic nature of design. And like many of the most successful designers working today, she isn't married to one style; rather, she's comfortable moving between contemporary and traditional—and points in between.

FROM: Seguin, Texas

LOCATED IN: Houston, Texas

INFLUENCES: Carlo Scarpa, Alvar Aalto, Louis Kahn, Rose Tarlow, Bunny Williams, and Victoria Hagan. Their outlooks, philosophies, romanticism, and aesthetics have made an indelible mark on me.

THE LOOK: Dynamic and classically current.

COLOR: I have an affinity for contrast, whether stark, like black and white, or more subdued, like charcoal and ivory. A perfectly neutral project has never been something I'm interested in

producing. Black is a timeless foundation that invites a well-placed dose of color.

KEY ELEMENT: Large-scale lighting, larger than you would typically think is appropriate, is a recurring theme in my interiors. The bigger, the better. If the ceiling is too low for a grand chandelier, then put it on the floor!

ALWAYS HAVE: Almost every room should have lots of chairs. I will never know enough people to simultaneously sit in the number of chairs I have in my home, at my studio, and in storage.

INSPIRATION: The Brion tomb and sanctuary by Carlo Scarpa, in San Vito d'Altivole, Italy, will always be inspirational for me. It is quiet, remote, thoughtful, and beautiful. The architecture, culture, and varied pace of life in Rome, Paris, Barcelona, London, Los Angeles, and New York. And art is equally inspiring: I love Marc Chagall (again, romantic!), Cy Twombly, and Leslie Parke and her realism, as well as Fairfield Porter, Willem de Kooning, and René Magritte because he's cheeky.

NEVER FORGET: Windows are of the utmost importance. I like to consider the interior moments, layouts, and circulation alongside framing beautiful views to the outdoors. Not only do window openings and window styles enhance the interior beautifully, they also artfully connect the home to its surroundings. My advice is to capture site-specific views with the interior plan in mind.

Unexpected playful touches make great choices for guest bedrooms. Here, a colorful settee purchased from Feliz Interiors Houston sits in front of six vintage encyclopedias hung gallery-style and interspersed with framed portraits.

OPPOSITE: A glinting Niermann Weeks chandelier, reminiscent of a gold bracelet, adorns the ceiling of this breakfast room. The vintage table was purchased from Carl Moore in Houston.

ABOVE: While designed for a young family to spend quality time together, this living room is also prepared for entertaining, with glamorous metallic touches.

RIGHT: For a homeowner with twin six-year-olds, a mudroom is a necessity. A stylized animal print makes a strong wallcovering, while the bench is upholstered in a playful polka-dot fabric by Caroline Z Hurley. A large-scale plaid marble floor provides the counterpoint. (left) A lively mix of color and pattern invigorates this dining room, which is grounded by a blue-and-white Gracie wallpaper. (right)

THE PARTNERS

> *"It's amazing what can happen if you take away what is unnecessary."*

LEE CAVANAUGH

> *Cullman & Kravis*

Lee Cavanaugh can trace her design career back to her Barbie Dreamhouse; she was obsessed with styling each room, paying the utmost attention to how each space was to be used. When her request for a canopy bed was ignored, she took apart her metal bed frame, added fabric and Christmas lights, and in mere moments created the bed of her dreams. This keen interest in design eventually led Cavanaugh to earning a degree in art and design from the University of Vermont, and then to studying art and architecture at Parsons School of Design in New York City.

Cavanaugh joined Cullman & Kravis as an intern in 1996, with a focus on textiles and fine art. Over the course of her career there, she learned all aspects of the interior design business. In 2013, she was named a partner in the firm.

The entry hall sets the tone for the palette throughout: Its white walls serve as the perfect backdrop for the clients' collection of photography and contemporary art. The high-gloss ceiling provides an additional bounce of light in this interior space. The clock artwork is by a group called Humans since 1982 and is titled *A Million Times*; it's a kinetic sculpture and functioning timepiece, and it was the very first work that the clients purchased for the apartment.

FROM: Boston, Massachusetts

LOCATED IN: New York, New York

INFLUENCES: If I had to choose the designer who had the most influence on my work, I would have to say Alberto Pinto. Oftentimes I find elements of his work reinterpreted in my own. His keen eye and flawless attention to detail are something I aspire to in my work. I am also inspired by the work of many French designers from the 1940s.

THE LOOK: Layered and eclectic, with a touch of glamour.

COLOR: I love color, and I am not afraid to use it! Neutrals often fall flat and can feel lifeless and dull without a pop of energetic color. When starting a new project, one of the very first conversations I have with my clients is about color. Most importantly, the overall color layout of a home needs to be cohesive and flow seamlessly from room to room, relating and complementing as you move through the home.

KEY ELEMENTS: Tchotchkes, art, and books. I am an avid collector of "things." *All* things. I am obsessed with art and sculpture. I find looking at a blank wall a complete bore. My friends make fun of me because there is not one empty space on any wall in my entire apartment. My tabletops display various collections of sculpture, art glass, and family photos. I love coffee-table books—they are piled under all of my console tables. I find inspiration and comfort being surrounded by things I am passionate about.

ALWAYS HAVE: Comfortable seating. More than just making a room look beautiful, you need to spend time thinking about how your clients will use and live in the rooms you design. Take a large living room: I like to think of my clients hosting a party, for which they will need various seating areas for guests to sit and talk comfortably and intimately. They will need surfaces to rest their drinks, plus layered lighting to highlight both the room's beauty and that of their guests.

INSPIRATION: The museums and culture in Paris, the architecture and fashion in New York City, and the visionary mood of Art Basel in Miami.

NEVER FORGET: What guarantees a successful room? Layout and lighting. I have been at many a friend's home for a dinner party, and after a nice meal and a lot of wine, we start to rearrange furniture and move lamps to add light!

OPPOSITE: A small bump-out in the master bedroom was transformed into a desk niche. The Sputnik-style desk is like a functional sculpture, with its geodesic orbs infusing a bit of whimsy.

TOP: The master bedroom, a tranquil oasis of white, blues, and creams, serves as the perfect backdrop for the mix of vintage and contemporary furnishings that range from 1940s Italian to midcentury American pieces to newly made custom commissions.

BOTTOM: To warm up the stone-and-nickel master bathroom, the designer chose a 1950s Italian chandelier and a sculptural vintage Fornasetti chair. Both bring a bit of personality to the pristine white backdrop.

> *"A house can be beautifully planned and decorated, but without proper lighting, it will never look its best."*

SARAH RAMSEY

> *Cullman & Kravis*

Sarah Ramsey grew up in a home filled with art and antiques, and visited antique stores and shows with her mother, a decorator, and her father, a passionate amateur collector. Ramsey started her career in the auction world, with an internship in Florence, Italy, then a gig at Weschler's in Washington, D.C., and ultimately a job at Sotheby's in New York City. She made the transition to the decorating world as Ellie Cullman's assistant at Cullman & Kravis, working her way up to partner over twelve years.

More than anything else, Ramsey credits her extensive travels for informing her design work. "I was pushed out the door by my parents at an early age, and that started my love of travel," she says. "I always pick up local art, ceramics, and sculpture when I'm in a new place." It's Ramsey's exposure to art and antiques, her love of experiencing other cultures, and her keen eye for color that make her rooms so successful.

THE LOOK: Tailored, edited, refined.

COLOR: I tend to run from the tonal white, beige, and gray palettes; I just can't seem to make those rooms work. I prefer lots of rich, saturated color! Teal, purple, orange, red, and leaf green: there's really not a color I dislike. And, of course, I love metallic finishes that provide silver and gold. One of my favorite ways to incorporate color is to use decorative paint to personalize a space. The possibilities are limitless, and it makes a big impact.

KEY ELEMENT: A really comfortable upholstered sofa. Nothing anchors a room better than a great place to sit and relax with friends and family.

ALWAYS HAVE: A variety of lighting. It is so important to use a mixture of sources in a room to achieve layered lighting. Ceiling lights, sconces, and lamps together not only properly light a room for day-to-day living, but also provide a warm and inviting ambience.

INSPIRATION: I fell in love with Asia on a trip to Indonesia, Malaysia, and Thailand in my twenties. I have always had a love for ethnic printed fabrics, and one day I will get to India! I also spent a year in London in Christie's education program. I soaked up anything and everything

FROM: Richmond, Virginia

LOCATED IN: New York, New York

INFLUENCES: Women's history is filled with inspiring, talented designers, and Ellie, from whom I have learned all the ropes, will influence designers for generations to come. I can't get enough of Alberto Pinto; I reference his work on every job. There are at least fifty sticky notes marking pages in his books in the office as we speak. I also love Brian J. McCarthy's work. He has mastered traditional, contemporary, and everything in between. I love how he can accessorize a room sparingly, but it still looks rich and interesting.

A custom walnut-and-bronze dining table anchors one end of the large loftlike space and is accented by the handblown-glass pendants by artisan Alison Berger. The vintage Art Deco dining chairs and Paolo Buffa buffet infuse the space with a sense of soul when combined with these newly made pieces.

English and never tired of visiting country houses. And, finally, I enjoy seeing how my contemporaries are approaching design.

NEVER FORGET: It is essential to have a floor plan that is both functional and comfortable. To ensure proper scale and proportion, it is critical to create an accurate, two-dimensional furniture layout prior to purchasing items.

OPPOSITE: An expansive corner window is framed on one side by a swath of juniper-green wool curtains. The custom shagreen games table, surrounded by Art Deco chairs, creates a cozy spot to look out at the hustle and bustle of New York City.

ABOVE: In the small foyer, there wasn't a lot of room for furniture. This petite transparent Giacometti-inspired console manages to keep the space visibly open, however. The addition of the 1960s red-glass mirror further opened up the room by reflecting the natural light coming through the doorway to the family room. (left) Located in a quiet corner, the office niche of the living room features a lacquer-and–brass inlay cabinet that creates a spot for the client to display her art books and vintage pottery collection. (right)

CLAIRE RATLIFF

> *Cullman & Kravis*

Having worked in the offices of Robert A. M. Stern and David Kleinberg, and now as a partner in the storied New York design firm Cullman & Kravis, Claire Ratliff certainly has an admirable design pedigree. But it was her mother's influence that set Ratliff on her path in the decorative arts. Ratliff remarks, "My mother is truly a self-taught genius. She has no formal training, but she was a voracious reader who studied books upon books about antiques, porcelain, architecture, and interiors. I always say that by the age of eleven, I had been to every antiques dealer and upholsterer in Texas. I couldn't have escaped this as a career path if I wanted to!"

Not only did Ratliff's mother teach her about antiques, she also taught her how to mix high and low and work within a budget, invaluable skills that Ratliff uses to this day.

In this vignette in the living room, a Robert Longo digital pigment print hangs above a William IV calamander-wood campaign chest. The unusual silver mounts add a glinting touch of modernity to this antique piece.

FROM: Austin, Texas

LOCATED IN: New York, New York

INFLUENCES: The year I spent living in London, attending the Inchbald School of Design, an interior and landscape design school just off Sloane Square. And Ellie Cullman. She is known as a traditionalist, but there is not a genre that she steers clear of. She has taught me how to take a classic approach to every style.

THE LOOK: Clean-lined, traditional rooms that are rooted in history but updated for today.

COLOR: I love bright colors. I'm obsessed with orange, from pumpkin to coral to burnt orange, and will attempt to pop it in any scheme that needs a little something.

KEY ELEMENT: A successful furniture plan. If it just looks pretty but doesn't function, what's the point?

ALWAYS HAVE: A few bargain flea-market finds. I love the thrill of the hunt, and even if a client has an open-ended budget, I get a kick out of finding that deal.

INSPIRATION: Historic cities and towns. This past summer, my family rented a house in Stonington, Connecticut, a tiny, charming coastal village. Visiting feels like taking a step back in time. And on a recent trip to Florence, Italy, there was inspiration everywhere! There is not a surface in Florence that has not been adorned. And the gilding! The whole city shines!

NEVER FORGET: Inspiration is everywhere, and even more so in this digital age. But it's important to remember that access and expertise are not synonymous.

LEFT: The expansive living room was transformed into a multipurpose space full of vintage finds mixed with custom contemporary pieces to create a relaxed yet modern bohemian vibe. Saturated colors draw your eyes around the room.

ABOVE: A 1940s orange club chair from a flea market sets the palette for this cheerful boy's room. An Hermès wool blanket on the bed and art glass on the dresser continue the color scheme.

163

ALYSSA URBAN

➤ *Cullman & Kravis*

Born and raised in New York City, Alyssa Urban grew up experiencing the rich, culturally diverse worlds of theater, art, music, architecture, and design. She visited many museums in New York as a child, but her favorites were smaller-scale museums like the Frick, located in the former home of nineteenth-century industrialist Henry Clay Frick. Thinking about what it was like to live in that beautiful space inspired Urban's future studies.

After studying interior design at the University of Wisconsin, Urban returned to New York to begin her career working in the field of television set design. The energy on set and the fast pace of TV was exciting and fun, but almost as quickly as the sets were designed and built, they were taken down. After a few years, Urban wanted to do something more lasting and made the switch to residential design. Following stints in hospitality and cruise ship design, she found her way to Cullman & Kravis, where she is now a partner. Each of these experiences have informed her refined aesthetic, which is marked by clean lines layered with color and decorative elements.

COLOR: I love to think about pops of color throughout a home, be it a band of color on the wall, colorful art, the use of color in fabrics, or painting an entire space one color.

KEY ELEMENTS: For visual interest, I like to add embroidered throw pillows and curtains, as well as decoratively painted walls.

ALWAYS HAVE: Handcrafted custom pieces created by skilled artisans. I was lucky enough to study abroad in Florence, Italy, where I was exposed to the history of art, as well as to skilled local craftspeople using materials like leather, wood, and textiles.

INSPIRATION: The 1993 film adaptation of Edith Wharton's *The Age of Innocence*—I'm still enthralled by the opulence and level of detail in the sets.

NEVER FORGET: Custom detailing. Embroidery, decorative painting, and one-of-a-kind pieces of furniture are the elements that make a room truly personal.

FROM: New York, New York

LOCATED IN: New York, New York

INFLUENCES: I have always admired Alberto Pinto, who is known for his grand and worldly creativity in very opulent settings. His attention to detail and his ability to seamlessly mix genres is incredibly inspiring.

THE LOOK: Comfortably sophisticated. An eclectic mix of traditional and modern.

To give this white kitchen a bit of personality and presence, a glass backsplash in vibrant turquoise was added. The vintage Venini glass pendants and the sculptural rush barstools further exemplify the strong mix of objects and surfaces in evidence throughout the home.

The family room, carved out of one end of the kitchen, is a welcoming, colorful mix of old and new. A custom vibrant purple velvet sofa, a 1950s American cloverleaf wooden coffee table, a 1970s glass-and-brass chandelier, and vintage-inspired lacquered dining chairs all live harmoniously together in this laid-back hangout space.

"Today's clients want to be involved in the process. People want a sense of ownership—the days of the hands-off client are over."

CALEB ANDERSON

› *Drake/Anderson*

Growing up in Texas, Caleb Anderson remembers his mother and grand-mother taking a keen interest in the décor of their homes, and he often found himself involved in their decisions. In high school he decorated his room to suit his taste. His favorite aunt owned a glamorous Georgian house outside of Dallas, which he marveled at when visiting. His interest led him to study interior design at Texas State University. His first real commission was for his aunt.

After graduating, Anderson applied for an internship with Jamie Drake of Drake Design Associates in New York. He got the position, and less than a year later found himself on staff at the firm. After a stint with the architect David Mann, Anderson opened his own firm in 2012. In 2015, Anderson merged his company with his former mentor's. Drake/Anderson mixes Drake's strong color sense and a focus on glamour with Anderson's more restrained, classical approach for rooms that are on point for the twenty-first century.

be purposeful and impactful with color, whether it is saturating a room with it or, in the case of my own apartment, eliminating it almost entirely. A room drenched in a single color in varying tones can be quite impactful. As much as I adore color, I also enjoy neutrals. My current apartment is completely neutral and I find it quite calming. With that said, I am constantly evolving and my next home will certainly have some color. It's fascinating how evocative color or the absence of color is in a room.

KEY ELEMENT: Art. A room is unfinished without it.

ALWAYS HAVE: An antique or vintage piece with personal meaning, even in the most contemporary projects. It is important to have that layer—it makes a house feel like a home and less like a furniture store or showroom.

INSPIRATION: I love to visit houses of the Gilded Age, historical palaces, and significant homes abroad. The Dolmabahçe Palace in Istanbul, the Musée Nissim de Camondo in Paris, and Villa Necchi Campiglio in Milan are a few of my favorites.

NEVER FORGET: To vary materials and textures. Glass on glass, wood on wood, stone on stone, and velvet on velvet don't work in my opinion. I would never put a glass vase on a glass table or a velvet pillow on a velvet sofa.

A glamorous Gabriel Scott chandelier and a custom wallcovering by Black Crow Studios were chosen to create this high-style New York City dining room, which reimagines the classic blue-and-white color scheme.

FROM: Austin, Texas

LOCATED IN: New York, New York

INFLUENCES: Billy Baldwin, George Stacey, Jacques Grange, Marc du Plantier, and Jean-Michel Frank. And, of course, Jamie Drake.

THE LOOK: Dynamically eclectic spaces that balance timelessness and modernity.

COLOR: I love color—rich colors that have a clarity, a single color contrasted with black and white. I always try to

OPPOSITE: A circular canvas by Karl Schrag from 1968 informs the color palette in this library, where a seafoam-green velvet sofa, metallic coffee table, and black-lacquered side chair complete the tableau. The *tulipiere* is by contemporary ceramic artist Matthew Solomon.

ABOVE: A custom-designed banquette provides ample seating in the corner of this living room, which is animated by a canvas by New York artist Melinda Hackett. Black and gold are employed throughout, and the baroque mirror is from the nineteenth century.

RIGHT: The breakfast nook includes a canvas by contemporary artist Susan Vecsey, known for her horizon-line paintings.

"Designing a home is like reading a novel— you never fully understand the characters until the very last page."

DAVID JOHN DICK

➤ *DISC Interiors*

Although David John Dick claims the architecture and contemporary Art and Craft movements of California as strong influences, he is also drawn to the richness of Southern interiors and their sense of comfort and tradition. Born in Ohio, Dick grew up in Memphis, Tennessee, and after attending university in Chicago and a stint in Scotland, he settled in California. Having lived in different parts of the United States and overseas has given him perspective on how location influences interiors. Dick explains, "My work is an attempt to make sense of the places where I have lived and traveled, a quest to blend my history and present."

Dick's personal aesthetic is based in craft, woodworking, and other works made by hand. He has a deep appreciation for Japanese and Shaker design and seeks to create spaces with elegance, restraint, and simplicity. Dick cofounded his firm, DISC Interiors, with his partner, Krista Schrock, in 2012. Dick appreciates minimalism in design and strong artistic statements, but also secretly loves the warmth and familiarity that comfortable and cozy rooms can bring.

THE LOOK: Calm, layered, and comfortable.

COLOR: As a whole, I'm drawn toward colors or tones that are faded and more neutral. In Los Angeles, the sunlight is so strong that neutral colors for interiors have a grounding balance with our natural terrain. I favor calm spaces and colors that soothe. I want my interior spaces to comfort, balance, and nourish.

KEY ELEMENT: Accessories bring final balance and movement to a room. Large pieces of stone or wood ground a space; bowls and vessels made of metal, ceramic, or stone add openness and light and are perfect for flowers or branches; and linen throws and candles are great for cold evenings.

ALWAYS HAVE: Every room must have function *and* purpose. There is a delight in designing rooms that are to be inhabited, not merely admired.

INSPIRATION: I'm inspired by ancient civilizations and how people lived in the past. I've been lucky enough to travel to China, Japan, Morocco, Russia, Europe, and ruins throughout Mexico. The ancient gardens, water towns, and ink paintings of China; the architecture and tilework of Fez, Morocco;

This Italian chandelier, designed by Giopato & Coombes, is reminiscent of bubbles drifting in space and served to bring a sense of wonder to this dining room in Pasadena, California. The leather-trimmed chairs stand in artful juxtaposition to an oak-and–blackened steel dining table.

FROM: Dayton, Ohio

LOCATED IN: Los Angeles, California

INFLUENCES: Charles Rennie Mackintosh, the Scottish architect, for his ability to mix modernism with the highly decorative, creating completely personal and imaginative spaces. Also, the Greene and Greene architectural firm. Like Mackintosh, Greene and Greene merged traditional Japanese woodworking with Arts and Crafts architecture in a very California way.

the stone carvings and scale of the
Mexican ruins; and woodworking
in Japanese architecture in Kyoto
continue to inspire me.

NEVER FORGET: Scale is of the
utmost importance. The proper scale
and placement of furniture, rugs,
lighting, and drapery are crucial to
the impact of a room.

The materials for the fireplace
wall in this informal living room
are balanced but asymmetrical,
combining a mix of concrete,
blackened steel, and oak beams.
The blackened-oak circular
coffee tables, leather recliner,
and custom sofa by DISC Interiors
are arranged casually to break
up the space.

KRISTA SCHROCK

> *DISC Interiors*

Looking back, Krista Schrock can see how growing up in rural western Pennsylvania influenced her design aesthetic. "My mom, grandmother, and aunts were makers: crafting, sewing, gardening, cooking, arranging flowers, and decorating," she says. "A general sense of aesthetics was strong in my household."

Schrock moved west to Los Angeles, where she pursued a degree, and subsequently a career, in graphic design. These years taught her about color, texture, scale, and spatial layout, but she began to crave something more tactile. The transition to interior design was a natural one. Schrock worked for notable design firms in Los Angeles, honing her love for textiles and vintage furniture design. She opened DISC Interiors with her partner, David John Dick, in 2012.

Schrock says their firm's aesthetic is always evolving, but it is focused on using natural materials such as wood, leather, and linen paired with iron or brass detailing. The result: quintessentially modern yet classic California-influenced rooms.

COLOR: Color is secondary to texture for me. I love mixing velvet, linen, and leather. I gravitate mostly toward neutrals, warm earth tones, and a generous amount of black as an accent.

KEY ELEMENT: I am an avid lover of vintage textiles, and I am always seeking out new textile ideas to inform a color palette.

ALWAYS HAVE: I prefer a less-is-more approach to accessories. The few essentials, to me, are great art books, collectibles from traveling, antique textile pillows, and a good ceramic or brass bowl. Less is definitely more.

INSPIRATION: Lately, I have been spending a lot of time looking at vintage furniture in old auction catalogs, which inspires many details in our own furniture line. My color palette is inspired by nature: fox fur, Icelandic horse manes, and bird feathers, to name a few.

NEVER FORGET: I think the mistake people make is with scale. Most people tend to scale down, and that is always a mistake. I say, go bigger! A bigger rug, a bigger chair—just go bigger!

FROM: Somerset, Pennsylvania

LOCATED IN: Los Angeles, California

INFLUENCES: I grew up in a small, rural town with a big Amish presence. I was strongly influenced by the simplicity of form of the Shaker and Amish styles, as well as their color palettes of creams and blacks. I also loved that each household item had a specific purpose; there was little ornamentation, just clean lines and natural materials.

THE LOOK: Warm minimalism.

Vintage Italian chairs surround a round travertine table with a brass top, lending a sense of history to this contemporary home office. The textured black grass-cloth wallpaper combines with the custom bleached-jute rug to bring in texture and warmth.

TOP: Twelve-foot-high ceilings and a massive sliding window highlight a mature and thriving tree just outside this airy kitchen. Caesarstone counters are worry-free for a family who loves to cook, while a pair of classic Danish pendants are suspended over the island.

BOTTOM: A composition of vertical and horizontal lines on the bookcase and window add interest in an otherwise serene bedroom. The built-in window seat provides the perfect perch for reading a book or a brief respite in the filtered sunlight.

OPPOSITE: In this dining room, an antique brass lantern with milk glass from Spain offers mood lighting in the evening that can be seen from the pool. The vintage Danish chairs were re-covered in a sage leather to blend into the lush scenery outside.

MATTHEW BEMIS

> *David Kleinberg Design Associates*

Matthew Bemis had a nomadic childhood, moving every few years. His father worked in the shoe industry, and took the family to Asia for the first time when Bemis was four years old; they followed production from country to country throughout his childhood. Bemis was exposed to contrasting cultures and vernaculars through his travels to Maine, South Korea, Massachusetts, Taiwan, Oregon, Japan, Los Angeles, Hong Kong, New Hampshire, and Vietnam. No matter the length of his stay, all of these places influenced his perspective on design.

Before joining Kleinberg's firm in 2012, Bemis worked for Etienne Coffinier and Ed Ku's firm, where he learned how to apply architectural principles to interiors and construction; for Thad Hayes, where he learned a respect for the history of both decoration and furniture; and for Peter Marino, who taught him to appreciate all the possibilities that are out there in terms of artists, artisans, and craftsman.

A coffered plaster ceiling was designed to provide space for recessed lighting in this paneled Park Avenue library. A glass-and-metal coffee table by contemporary artist Fredrikson Stallard floats on a lush geometric-patterned rug. Custom upholstered pieces provide ample seating.

FROM: Lawrence, Massachuesetts

LOCATED IN: New York, New York

INFLUENCES: Like most designers, I look at traditional decoration as a foundation. But after that, I look to more recent designers who make history applicable to today. For me—and many, many others—those designers are Jacques Grange and Alberto Pinto. I always find their work to be historically significant while still appealing and functional in the modern world. And, of course, David Kleinberg.

THE LOOK: Refined, timeless, and tailored.

COLOR: In most of my projects, color is an accent and used to set a mood, but it is typically not dominant or the statement. I try to create a neutral or timeless foundation where colors are incorporated as accents for tone or context. Inspiration for a color direction really varies from project to project. Sometimes it is vernacular and very specific to the location, site, or existing details. In some instances, it starts with a beautiful print or textile and branches out from there. Other times, it comes directly from the client and their feedback or inspiration material.

KEY ELEMENTS: Large, neutral upholstery pieces, geometric area rugs, and a special handwoven textile—even if it's just a pillow. It helps keep things from becoming too static.

ALWAYS HAVE: Every room needs a bit of leather or suede. And metal details, whether in the architecture or on a piece of furniture. It adds a jewelry-like quality to the space.

INSPIRATION: Lucian Freud and Egon Schiele made me realize for the first time that art can be more than something that is just pretty to look at. Their work provoked emotion, thought, and intrigue. Fine interior design has the ability to elicit the same response in those who inhabit or visit a space.

NEVER FORGET: To be sure you have prioritized the most important items on your wish list. Whether or not a home feels luxurious depends upon perception. Sacrifices might have to be made, but in the end, if you have fulfilled your, or your client's, most important desires, that sense of luxury will prevail.

An Italian wing chair from Bernd Goeckler adds a sculptural element in front of exotic-wood paneling. The adjacent entryway is clad with plaster walls that have a hint of silver leaf. The floor is patterned limestone.

SEAN MATIJEVICH

> *David Kleinberg Design Associates*

From his earliest days, Sean Matijevich remembers wanting to be an artist. His interest in design was sparked by visits to the local fabric store, where his mother would look at pattern books while he and his brother would wander the aisles. There were always projects going on in the family home, whether it was wallpapering the dining room or reupholstering the living room sofa.

By the time Matijevich reached high school, he was hungry to see the world. A spur-of-the-moment trip led him to fall in love with New York City, where he landed his first design job with Stephen Sills via an ad in the *New York Times*. Matijevich recalls Sills as a great teacher and master of magic making. A few years later, he interviewed with—and was ultimately hired by—another design hero, David Kleinberg. Matijevich's rooms incorporate Kleinberg's curated and restrained aesthetic, and carry on the legacy of Kleinberg's mentors, Albert Hadley and Sister Parish.

Recessed into a corner of the master bedroom, this seating area is the perfect spot for coffee or an afternoon read. A set of Italian midcentury nesting tables sits between the chairs. Neutral textiles keep the light-filled space from feeling cluttered.

OVERLEAF: A neutral palette punctuated by dark-navy accents allows the artwork to be the star in this expansive living room, which features works by Gerhard Richter, Andy Warhol, and Donald Judd. The skirted console tables were unconventionally tailored in leather.

FROM: Rochester, New York

LOCATED IN: New York, New York

INFLUENCES: Maxime Old, Paul Dupré-Lafon, and Samuel Marx are three designers whose work I reference again and again. They took classic forms and reinterpreted the lines with fresh eyes to bring them forward.

THE LOOK: Classically based, but approachable.

COLOR: Rich color is something that always inspires me. Color is everywhere, and I never tire of it: the brilliant—and often unusual—colors of lacquered Parisian doors, the neutral stone floors of Rome, the deep greens of English gardens, the beautiful blues of the Adriatic, the autumnal reds and golds of New England, and the cool gray and silver of the concrete jungle in New York City.

KEY ELEMENT: Comfort. You can walk into the most beautiful rooms and never want to return if they are so precious and curated that you are afraid to touch anything. My own residence is like a lab, as my husband will tell you, and things move around frequently.

ALWAYS HAVE: I've always had a great love of nature, and to this day one can find any number of rocks, dried twigs, bird nests, or dried leaves on the tabletops of my own apartment—right next to lacquer boxes and glazed ceramics.

INSPIRATION: I'm often inspired by a work of fine art. I remember the first project I ever did for David Kleinberg was based on *Queen Isabel, Standing*, a 1631 portrait of the monarch by Diego Velázquez; it's a painting I adore. The rich ochers of the background; the midnight blues of her gown, with its intricate silver beadwork; and the deep chocolates of her hair make the porcelain white and pink of her face stand out in the most glorious fashion. More recently, I was inspired by a graffiti tour of Bushwick.

NEVER FORGET: The first discussion every designer needs to have with his or her client should begin with the question "How do you see your life in the new space?" The answer, about how the client wants to inhabit his or her home, charts the course for a successful collaboration.

"Although there will always be a need for entertaining areas, people are leaning toward more relaxed interiors, but still filled with luxurious things."

LANCE SCOTT

➤ *David Kleinberg Design Associates*

Lance Scott's grandfather was an attorney, but his real interest was in architecture; in fact, after he found success in the law, he went on to design and build all of the family's residences. So from his earliest memories, Scott was surrounded by floor plans, and his grandfather would always ask for his opinion. As an adult, Scott himself took a circuitous route to interior design: he first studied public relations at Southern Methodist University, in Dallas, then switched gears like his grandfather to do post-graduate work in the architecture program at the University of Texas.

Scott soon found his way to New York City, and to a job with David Kyner, one of the co-owners of Howard Kaplan Antiques. Kyner mentored Scott on buying trips, encouraging him to explore museums and galleries.

In 2006, Scott began his tenure at David Kleinberg Design Associates. He will never forget the question Kleinberg asked him in his interview: "When you're walking down the street, what store windows do you look at? You never know where inspiration will be found." To this day, Scott always makes time to stop and look.

THE LOOK: Contemporary with a touch of refined glamour.

COLOR: For the most part, I gravitate toward cooler rather than warmer colors and neutrals. When using a color, I prefer muted tones: soft blues and celadon greens, pale lavenders, and sherbet colors. When approaching color on a new project, I always look to the clients' appearance for input. Seeing the way they put themselves together can tell you a lot about what colors they lean toward and how saturated they prefer them.

KEY ELEMENT: Crisply tailored upholstery with discreet dressmaker details.

ALWAYS HAVE: Some lacquerwork, whether on the walls, on a table, or in a simple accessory. And some shine, such as rock-crystal pieces, fractured resin, palladium leaf, or a new rose-gold cerused finish on an old oak cabinet.

INSPIRATION: Photography is a major inspiration for me and is also a good analogy for the way I approach my work. The composition of an image, the color, the lighting, the layering or lack thereof. I enjoy works by Diane Arbus, Richard Avedon, Robert Mapplethorpe, Andreas Gursky, Marilyn Minter, and especially Thomas Ruff.

A reverse painted–glass backsplash by Brooklyn artist Vesna Bricelj interjects an organic sensibility into this angular, masculine bar. The cabinets are ebonized mahogany, French-polished to a high-gloss shine.

FROM: San Antonio, Texas

LOCATED IN: New York, New York

INFLUENCES: Renzo Mongiardino, for the layers of pattern and texture; Syrie Maugham, for the touches of glamour; and couturiers like Charles James, Christian Dior, Valentino Garavani, and Oscar de la Renta, for the exquisite finishing details that translate over to the layers of any interior space.

NEVER FORGET: Powder rooms are always a great place to be daring. Try dramatic dark walls with a cool light fixture and art, mixtures of metal and stone, or a subtle texture on the walls. In a larger space, it is nice to have a place for someone to sit or place a handbag, so a small, artful chair with an interesting table could be a great way to fill a corner. If the room is large enough, use a dressing table with a mirror. Powder rooms are primarily for guests, so they should feel inviting but also unexpected.

A pair of sculptural bronze club chairs, upholstered in a navy-blue mohair, complement the suede-and-chrome benches in the foreground of this sitting room. The artwork at right is by Cy Twombly; the bronze beach ball is by artist Sherrie Levine.

> *"Good proportions speak to one another and complement one another. They do not overwhelm, and they move the eye around the room."*

SCOTT SLOAT

> *David Kleinberg Design Associates*

New York–based designer Scott Sloat may have grown up outside Little Rock, Arkansas, but his interest in design was first ignited by family trips to the timeless Southern cities of Savannah, Georgia; Charleston, South Carolina; and Natchez, Mississippi. After college, Sloat interned with Georg Andersen Associates in Arkansas, a design firm with clients locally and in New York City. "It gave me a foundation in building excellent client relationships and business practices," Sloat says.

After graduating from the Fashion Institute of Technology in 1995 with a degree in interior design, Sloat joined Robert A. M. Stern Architects. There he worked directly with Raul Morillas, who instilled in him a sense of fantasy and glamour in design, and with Bob Stern, who promoted a strong sense of design integrity, proportion, and classical references. In 2000, he joined David Kleinberg Design Associates. Through Kleinberg, Sloat joins the lineage of Parish-Hadley and incorporates their sense of restrained luxury and gracious living into every project.

COLOR: All of us at DKDA are descendants of the Parish-Hadley family. To quote Albert Hadley, "Beige is atmosphere. It's bisque, it's ivory, it's cream, it's stone, it's toast, it's cappuccino. It's, well, it's magic." A neutral palette allows for a timeless interior, one that doesn't follow a trendy color that will fall out of fashion in a year or two. Anyone can throw a bunch of colorful fabrics in a room and call it design, but being able to curate a neutral palette that allows for chic, timeless interiors takes skill.

KEY ELEMENT: Proper proportion and scale are crucial to creating a successful room. Correct scale can be the difference between a room that screams off-key or one that sings in harmony.

ALWAYS HAVE: A mix of humble and luxurious materials: good woven textures, striped fabrics, great taffeta, contrast welts on upholstery, and custom furniture from artisans such as W. P. Sullivan or Laurence Montano.

INSPIRATION: Inspiration for my work comes from many sources. Travel, art shows, and antiques inspire color, shape, and form in interiors, while fashion shows inspire couture detailing, whether on curtains, a piece of furniture, or an architectural element.

FROM: Conway, Arkansas

LOCATED IN: New York, New York

INFLUENCES: Albert Hadley, David Adler, Henri Samuel, Samuel Marx, and Billy Baldwin are all great historical designers, and their mixing of fabrics, colors, and furnishings continues to inform my design decisions.

THE LOOK: Curated luxury, sophisticated yet comfortable, that is always a reflection of the client.

A monumental canvas by artist Mark Bradford takes pride of place in this white dining room. White-lacquered chairs, upholstered in a woven horsehair, sit on four striped rugs that were sewn together to create a graphic moment.

LEFT: A subtle repetition of linear patterns creates visual interest in this master bedroom. The chrome-and–ebonized mahogany bed and the leather-faced armoire were custom designed. The painting is by John Currin.

ABOVE: The gentleman's closet design was based on a retail store the client frequents. Brushed-oak cabinetry with open fronts give an at-a-glance view. The broadloom carpet marks the transition from the adjacent bath.

NEVER FORGET: A master bedroom must be serene; it's the last refuge for escape from today's pressures. Think of what you want to wake up to visually; purple ikat walls may not be the most peaceful view in the morning for most people. Other important elements include good lighting for reading, with lighting controls mounted discreetly at the bedside so that one does not have to leave the bed; blackout shades; nightstands with drawers for remotes; and the most comfortable down-filled upholstery.

CATHERINE OLASKY

➤ *Olasky & Sinsteden*

Catherine Olasky's father gave her a biography of Sister Parish while she was in college, and after reading the first few chapters, Catherine knew she wanted to be a decorator. So after graduating with a fine arts degree from Auburn University, she moved to New York to attend Parsons School of Design and pursue an internship with Bunny Williams.

"After a great deal of persistence on my part, Bunny's brilliant office manager agreed to interview me, and that was the career break of a lifetime," Olasky says. "I spent five amazing years working for Bunny, and then, in 2006, I moved to London to learn a different, equally fascinating model of traditional decorating by working for Roger Jones at Sibyl Colefax & John Fowler for four fantastic years." Olasky reconnected with Max Sinsteden during this period; they had met in New York via a shared mentor José Carlino. Their friendship led to the formation of their partnership in 2009.

In the entry hall of an 1840 home in Essex, Connecticut, Olasky & Sinsteden installed a custom Swedish-style flatweave carpet, loomed in Nantucket, on the stairs. The runner picks up the colors of a custom mural by Scott Waterman in the dining room beyond. The original newel post was French-polished.

FROM: Dallas, Texas

LOCATED IN: New York, New York; Houston, Texas; London, England

INFLUENCES: Obviously, I've been influenced by the decorators for whom I've worked. Bunny Williams taught me about color, fabrics, scale, lighting, and how to run a project. While working at Colefax, I learned about the importance of distilling ideas, paring back to what's essential, nuance, the play of masculine strength with feminine flourishes, and the postwar ethos of using simple, abundant materials gloriously reincarnated. Thinking of historical designers, I'm influenced by John Fowler, Sister Parish, and Albert Hadley.

THE LOOK: Traditional, detailed, and sophisticated.

COLOR: Color is about balance. If you use it all in one place, like an intensely pigmented plaster finish, you have to hit the brakes on the rest of the space. For example, a neutral space can handle strong-colored ceramic lamps and bright art. But the fun is sometimes working in the middle of the spectrum and fiddling with the balance until a palette *sings*. Colors have to be felt; it's very much a process of weighing how much you want to feel each one within a scheme.

KEY ELEMENT: Good lighting. I prefer natural light, but light from many "horizons" within a room is crucial. Whether from the ceiling, walls, floor, or tabletop, light needs to give a room the right brightness to accomplish a particular task, or the softness to relax and unwind.

ALWAYS HAVE: Antique carpets; brown wood furniture; details, details, details; Charles Beckley mattresses; and books.

INSPIRATION: I love to visit and learn from historic homes, which I view as a kind of anthropological study of people over time. How was each

room actually used? How does a floor plan hold up over time? What pieces have stayed, and what has changed? I'm also inspired by the painted finishes of Drottningholm Palace in Sweden, and early American furniture and homes.

NEVER FORGET: Good design is more accessible than ever, but it requires careful thought to put it all together. And as with many things, the more options you have, the harder it is to make choices.

To maintain a sense of the smaller scale of a historic home, Olasky & Sinsteden worked with the architect to divide the kitchen into two halves using architectural detailing and paint-color changes. A reproduction Connecticut tiger-maple kitchen table by cabinetmaker Peter Van Beckum provides additional prep space and a place for casual meals while not feeling like a kitchen island. Eighteenth-century Dutch tiles above the stove pick up colors in the newly built mudroom in the distance.

> *"A room without a sense of its owner is devoid of a soul."*

MAX SINSTEDEN

➤ *Olasky & Sinsteden*

Max Sinsteden describes himself as a little precocious. In high school, he began working with Lynne Einsel, C.O.O. of David Easton; he ended up spending four summers there as an intern. While attending Drew University, Sinsteden had a summer internship with Charlotte Moss, who asked if he would like to take a year off to help her and her team build out her townhouse store. He jumped at the chance and became hooked on interior design as a career. After several years working on and off for Moss, Sinsteden then pursued an internship in London with the Victoria and Albert Museum, where he reconnected with fellow designer Catherine Olasky, whom he had met in New York.

The pair hit it off and decided their individual decorating visions and work styles were different yet complementary enough to make for a great partnership. Ten years later, Olasky & Sinsteden has established itself as one of the country's best "new traditional" design firms.

FROM: Hartford, Connecticut

LOCATED IN: New York, New York and Houston, Texas

INFLUENCES: When working for David Easton, I learned the power of the floor plan and the importance of architecture. At Easton's office, José Carlino helped me see architectural interior elements with glamour and bold simplicity. Charlotte Moss also heavily influences my work. Her rooms are full of layers, with no detail too small. I endeavor to do the same. And Moss is a proponent of sublime femininity, which I also appreciate. I'm also influenced by designers Renzo Mongiardino, Bill Blass, and Roger Banks-Pye.

Olasky & Sinsteden used the shape of a pair of mirrors, from Carlton Hobbs, as inspiration for the over-embroidered leading edges on the curtains. The client's antique chair, from Russborough House, is covered in a custom woven damask. An important nineteenth-century woodwork picture hangs above a reclaimed period brownstone fire surround.

THE LOOK: Traditional, detailed, and sophisticated.

COLOR: It's hard to ever rule out any one color; it seems there is always somewhere or some context that a particular color will work in. The thrill of finding the "ugly" color or the "never in a thousand years" color and then thinking of the right context for it is exciting.

KEY ELEMENT: Furnishings that reflect a client's personality. Whether modern or traditional, make sure there are objects, art, fabrics, or furnishings that reflect who lives there.

ALWAYS HAVE: Trims, interlining in curtains, down-filled upholstery, gently vibrant colors, layers of lighting, and custom lampshades

INSPIRATION: I'm inspired by the gardens of Gertrude Jekyll and Russell Page, visits to historic hotels, and museums. I'm also inspired by design in Ireland, such as Castletown House, Desmond Guinness's house, Abbeyleix House, Curraghmore House, and most of all, the Casino at Marino. Back home, I'm infatuated with sailboats and the New England coast.

NEVER FORGET: In design, I think it's very important to respect practicality, especially when it comes to lighting, comfort, and durability. Rooms are meant to be lived in as much as they are to be admired.

TOP: Paneling designed by architect Robert Orr is painted in milk paint. A nineteenth-century ship model on the shelves speaks to the house's location.

BOTTOM: A rag rug is braided with the same check seen throughout the guest apartment. (left) A reclaimed soapstone sink in the powder room doubles as a great place to arrange flowers. (right)

OPPOSITE: In a single-room guest apartment, Olasky & Sinsteden utilized one fabric to unify the space.

> *"I feel connected to cultures that seek meaning through art and design—the continuity of artistic expression, the human impulse to paint a nature scene, or decorate a water pitcher."*

DAVID KAIHOI

➤ *Redd Kaihoi*

Born and raised in Minnesota, David Kaihoi studied art and art education at Bethel University in St. Paul, where he discovered a passion for making ceramic sculpture and mixed-media collage. In 2002, Kaihoi followed another love, his wife, to New York City. Living in the East Village, he continued making sculpture in his Chinatown studio while working for the art installation firm ILevel. It was the installation work that formally introduced him to the world of decoration and design, working alongside leading tastemakers of the day and exposing him to the finest private collections and interiors in New York. "Imagine starting your day at a Park Avenue penthouse with Mario Buatta, hanging a collection of Ming dynasty porcelain on satin upholstered walls," Kaihoi says. "It was an incredible firsthand education in all styles of decorating, not to mention an important experience working on high profile projects." A favorite client was the acclaimed designer Miles Redd. Their mutual respect resulted in a job offer.

In ´2007, Kaihoi joined Redd's eponymous firm and became his right-hand man, all the while honing his own unique vision in the design world. a fierce blend of downtown sensibility and refined uptown taste. In 2019, Redd announced Kaihoi as a partner and renamed the company Redd Kaihoi.

This vignette features a range of textures and tailored lines: silver grass-cloth walls; a velvet-covered Vladimir Kagan sofa, a pillow made from an African textile, and a plant in a rustic terra-cotta pot.

FROM: Willmar, Minnesota

LOCATED IN: New York, New York

INFLUENCES: The Giacometti brothers, Cy Twombly, Anni Albers, Donald Judd, Frances Elkins, François Catroux, Jean-Michel Frank, Renzo Mongiardino.

THE LOOK: Reconstructed traditionalism, bold pattern, and repetition.

COLOR: I approach color like weights on a scale and use it to push and pull the balance of a room. Tone, texture, density, and sheen all contribute to the weight of a color. I look for unlikely pairs that have a similar weight and use them as equals. For example, a small red painting may have the same weight as a large mahogany bookcase, and they might be used to anchor opposite ends of a room.

KEY ELEMENT: Handmade things. I love objects with signs of a living process, a quality that connects an object to a human hand; a spontaneous decision, an uneven patina . . . even a mistake.

ALWAYS HAVE: Repeated pattern, variety of texture, custom upholstery, and clear-eyed color.

INSPIRATION: I visited Petra once as a student many years ago and have never really recovered. The classical architecture carved into the rugged landscape is the height of sophistication. Its artistic engineering makes it a wonder of the world, but its physical beauty and mystical presence are what I will never forget.

NEVER FORGET: Be kind to your art and give it whatever it needs to remain autonomous. Some work wants to be alone in a wash of empty space, while other pieces benefit from good company in tight quarters. Never mind strict rules about height or hierarchy—trust your gut and hang things where they feel good.

TOP: Pink heron wallpaper makes a statement in the powder room.

BOTTOM: In this kitchen, the ceiling and cabinetry were painted in celadon lacquer. The antique Turkish rug creates contrast.

RIGHT: This garden-level bedroom in an eclectic townhouse balances a casual mix: Kaihoi's own Weeping Pine wallpaper for Schumacher, a Jean Royère—inspired bed faux-finished by Agustin Hurtado, and geometric-shaped Moroccan rugs cut to fit the space.

NOAH TURKUS

> *Weiss Turkus*

Noah Turkus developed a keen interest in design while watching his parents renovate their kitchen. He saw firsthand how material selection could transform a space. Small obsessive details, like designing hand-painted Italian tiles, grew into a burgeoning curiosity about color theory. Later, he fell hard for interior design during a summer internship, where he began refining his eye for textile and furniture selection.

Turkus met his future business partner, Lindsay Weiss, at the University of Pennsylvania. Their paths crossed again a few years later, when they both worked at Haynes-Roberts. Timothy Haynes and Kevin Roberts had a profound impact on both Turkus and Weiss; they inspired their style and taught them skills they utilize every day.

However, it is their parents whom Turkus and Weiss credit most for their shared appreciation for interior architecture and design. Turkus says, "Our education leading up to the Weiss Turkus collaboration began long before our formal training. Both of our families held attention to detail as sacred in their design of our childhood homes, and those homes have become such a useful experiential touchstone for our own designs."

A canvas by American contemporary artist Dale Weiss hangs in the living room of a New York City apartment. The organic, sculptural lamp is by Mirena Kim Ceramics, and the neutral sofa is by Baker.

FROM: Washington, D.C.

LOCATED IN: New York, New York

INFLUENCES: Lindsay and I are influenced by other designers, both historical and contemporary. Pierre Yovanovitch, Kelly Wearstler, and India Mahdavi are a few notables who continue to impress us with their bold moves and innovative custom furniture designs.

THE LOOK: Unexpected, crisp, and harmonious.

COLOR: I tend toward higher amounts of contrast, whether through interlocking complementary colors or simply by mixing textures with similar hues, such as using a supple wool sateen next to a rougher nubby tweed. This quality of graded contrast prevents a space from becoming lifeless or dull.

KEY ELEMENT: Every successful room needs a well-selected mix of materials. By this, I mean the combination of textiles with metal, wood, stone, leather, or lacquer.

ALWAYS HAVE: Luxurious materials and eclectic vintage finds.

INSPIRATION: I always find color inspiration from art. After visiting Manhattan's Chelsea galleries, I come home humming with color ideas. Theatrical and film set design also fascinates me, as do commercial spaces, mainly restaurants and hotels. When beginning a project, Lindsay and I rely on the alchemic process of throwing a lot of disparate ideas into the pot to see how they play together. The reality is that we are constantly seeking new ideas and inspiration.

NEVER FORGET: To target the exact right number of pieces for a space and avoid extraneous decor. Fewer pieces, stronger pieces. A successful project is one where we have curated an assemblage of pieces that look like they were collected over years and not mere months. This reads as soulful, and reflects a client's character and personality.

ABOVE: A custom radiator cover was extended to accommodate a window seat and fitted with a cushion in the master bedroom. The painting is by Brad Greenwood; the table lamp is by Christopher Spitzmiller.

RIGHT: A vintage Danish table-and-chairs set was purchased at a junk shop, then the table was stained darker and the chairs were lacquered in a deep blue. The canvases are by Brad Greenwood; the light fixture is by Gabriel Scott.

"The process of layering begins with the architectural detailing and is strengthened with furniture and furnishings."

LINDSAY WEISS

➤ *Weiss Turkus*

From an early age, Lindsay Weiss was exposed to the aesthetics of art and design in her mother's painting studio, where she created her first works of art—paintings, drawings, and elaborate book-report covers. She was constantly learning how to establish a visual language for the three-dimensional space around her. Her background in all areas of artistic expression, along with her growing curiosity about the built world, made the study and practice of architecture a natural evolution in her career path.

Both Weiss and her business partner, Noah Turkus, had the opportunity to travel at a young age and to become aware of how different cultures shape residential spaces. Their own work reflects exactly this. Perhaps the greatest takeaway from the similarity between their upbringings is their mutual desire to continue building on these mem-ories and to be open and curious about opportunities and experiences to inspire their work.

Kelly Wearstler's inspirational empire—she has modernized Deco and glam and made them approachable without losing any sophistication along the way.

THE LOOK: Layered, elegantly playful, eclectic.

COLOR: The consideration of color goes beyond a paint deck. I use primary construction materials like wood, stone, brick, and marble to add contrast and texture to our project palettes. I am obsessed with finding some incredible, expressive slab of marble that can capture a quality that our fabrics and paint cannot. We often use color as a balancing agent to make sure that the architectural materials do not overweigh a certain area. Positive space, negative space, quality of light, and presence of shadow will all affect how that color is seen.

KEY ELEMENT: Client interaction. Today's clients have a point of view and want to be educated and part of the process. They all bring to the table interesting living patterns and family dynamics. Their personal nuances help sculpt and refine the style and shape of the spaces that Noah and I design for them so that they can begin living in them on their terms.

ALWAYS HAVE: Every successful room needs to have different levels of scale to keep one's eye bouncing around in

FROM: Los Angeles, California

LOCATED IN: New York, New York

INFLUENCES: Jean Louis Deniot's restrained palette and his wonderful friction between the modern and the traditional influenced our work. Carlo Scarpa taught me the value of framing an architectural moment, and also how to create a detail over a range of scales. The art island of Naoshima, Japan, where I finally understood Tadao Ando and the effectiveness of a simple idea, as well as the tactile draw of natural materiality and how natural light can shape the focus of a space. And last,

Walls were taken down to open up the original galley kitchen, and a Carrara-marble waterfall peninsula was added for additional work space. The pendant light was creatively notched into the shelves above the bar.

an interested way. When we are adding layers to the room, it's the scale shift between architectural details, decorative objects, patterns, lighting, and furniture that keeps the room from becoming overwhelming—or underwhelming.

INSPIRATION: As an architect, I find inspiration in materials—how they are traditionally used, their construction properties and limits, and using them in unexpected ways.

NEVER FORGET: The way to sidestep spaces that lack interest is to focus continuously on fine levels of detailing. How does the profile of a door casing relate to the shape of a cabinet door across the room? How can integral or decorative pulls be added to a piece of millwork for that extra feature that reads bespoke? How are materials carried through a room, and then from that room to contiguous spaces. Our living spaces, just like ourselves, never exist in isolation. They are reflections of each other.

A geometric color-blocked rug, fashioned from wool, nylon, and silk, was designed in Photoshop and made in a custom workroom. It informed the color palette throughout the apartment. At the window is a pair of chairs by Jaime Hayon; the solo lounge chair is by Neri & Hu for De La Espada.

ELIZABETH M. LAWRENCE

➤ *Bunny Williams Interior Design*

Elizabeth M. Lawrence studied photography in college, and she went on to teach it before realizing her true interest was in interior design. So, she took an introductory class. She says, "I fell in love with it all and quickly realized I had been an interior designer from birth, building dollhouses and painting fabric for the furniture." So she moved to New York City to study at the New York School of Interior Design.

After her first year of school, Lawrence knew she needed work experience, and her mother suggested she send her résumé to Bunny Williams, which Lawrence did even though she had no hope of being hired. Fourteen years later, having risen through the ranks from intern to assistant designer to senior designer, Lawrence is now a partner in her mentor's firm. Together, Williams and Lawrence continue a legacy of design learned when Williams worked for the legendary firm Parish-Hadley.

Melon-colored Venetian plaster walls and a custom decorative floor set the tone in this entryway. The pair of George II gilt-wood console tables with sienna-hued marble tops took time to find, but the searching paid off. They are topped with Italian glass table lamps from 1950. Lawrence had the Queen Anne-style mirrors custom made by Dennis & Leen; the 1920s American neoclassical bronze pendant from David Duncan is the perfect scale and gives off nice light in the evening during parties.

FROM: Wilmington, Delaware

LOCATED IN: New York, New York

INFLUENCES: I love all the great historic decorators, such as Sister Parish and Dorothy Draper. I am particularly captivated by Nancy Lancaster and John Fowler: their style, their lives, and their rooms were always glamorous. My first apartment in New York City—a small studio with an English vibe and chintz to spare—was definitely influenced by them.

THE LOOK: Traditional mixed with modern.

COLOR: I think you have to approach color based on what feels best to the client. Some people want a more calming, neutral palette, and others are ready to go full force with saturated colors. Personally, I prefer when a great color is mixed with neutrals. If the rug has a lot of colors, maybe the walls are neutral and some of the furniture picks up colors from the rug. It is about striking the right balance.

KEY ELEMENT: A room without books doesn't feel as much like a home to me. I love going to someone else's home and seeing the books they have; I think it tells a lot about a person. It is also a fun way to learn about new books for my own collection.

ALWAYS HAVE: At least one or two upright chairs that aren't too deep. Deep sofas and chairs are comfortable and great for lounging, but they are not always so easy to get in and out of, especially as people get older. Also, a good throw is always appreciated for a nap.

INSPIRATION: The old homes and antiques stores my mother dragged me to as a child. They gave me a deep appreciation for history, and that is reflected in my work. And, of course, I'm inspired by Bunny Williams. I have learned and grown in the design industry because of my experience with her.

NEVER FORGET: Everyone needs a comfortable reading chair with a lamp and small table for a book, as well as a place to plug in a cell phone.

OPPOSITE: The real showstoppers of this dining room are the pair of deep blue Italian vases circa 1800 that sit on Italian marble pedestals. They add great scale to the space and accentuate the ceiling height. An early-1800s English table, a late-eighteenth-century neoclassical Anglo-Irish mantelpiece, and a gilded English mirror circa 1840 complete the tableau.

TOP: In this library, Lawrence worked with a local wood finisher to get the pine walls a rich color without being too red. The traditional nature of the room is offset by a great modern rug from Warp & Weft. The curtains are simple panels made special with an embroidered edge. Beautiful antiques, such as the Asian-style red-lacquered coffee table, mix with modern pieces like the end tables on either side of the sofa.

BOTTOM: In the breakfast room, a Gracie wallpaper makes a connection to the garden outside. Furthering the effect is a chandelier of oxidized-metal leaves found in England that has a great scale and feeling. (left) The guest bedroom walls are upholstered in a Claremont fabric, which gives the room a cozy and quiet feeling. The same fabric is used on the window treatments. A simple wool rug from Doris Leslie Blau keeps the room from being too busy and balances all the pattern on the walls and curtains. The bed linens were made in Italy. (right)

ACKNOWLEDGMENTS

I would like to thank Charles Miers and Rizzoli New York for their continued faith in my work.

I would like to thank my literary agent, William Clark; my editor, Kathleen Jayes; the book's copyeditor, Jennifer Milne; the book's designer, Susi Oberhelman; and my publicist at Rizzoli, Jessica Napp.

I would like to thank my supporting friends, Anthony Costa, John DesLaurier, Brian Gorman, Justin Hambrecht, David Hamm, Abby Kaufmann, Patrick Key, Joey Grant Luther, Matthew Marsh, Jimmy O'Brien, Joe Putignano, Frank Quinn, Joel Robare, Daniel Rosado, and Alan Rohwer.

I would like to thank my mother, Ann Yost, for teaching me perseverance and that anything is possible if you put your mind to it.

And finally, I would like to thank my partner, Todd Lattimore, for helping me shine.

CREDITS

First published in the United States of America in 2019 by
Rizzoli International Publications, Inc.
300 Park Avenue South
New York, NY 10010
www.rizzoliusa.com

Copyright © 2019 Carl Dellatore

Publisher: Charles Miers
Senior Editor: Kathleen Jayes
Design: Susi Oberhelman
Production Manager: Kaija Markoe
Managing Editor: Lynn Scrabis

Printed in China

2019 2020 2021 2022 / 10 9 8 7 6 5 4 3 2 1

ISBN: 9780847865154
Library of Congress Control Number: 2019939993

Visit us online:
Facebook.com/RizzoliNewYork
Twitter: @Rizzoli_Books
Instagram.com/RizzoliBooks
Pinterest.com/RizzoliBooks
Youtube.com/user/RizzoliNY
Issuu.com/Rizzoli